Frank D'Andraia
Editor

The Academic Library Director: Reflections on a Position in Transition

This collection of essays reflecting on the role of the academic library director as we move to the 21st century is an important contribution to the literature. Written from a broad perspective the essays speak to libraries of all sizes.

Kobulnicky's article is a must read for anyone anticipating taking on the role of the acting director. It addresses a gap in the literature and provides useful insights as well as some practical suggestions. The articles by Martin and Brittingham are useful complements for those libraries in transition. Search committees especially will want to read these as they consider what kind of library leader will best meet their future needs. Martin in particular weaves the thinking of the management literature into the library environment.

The articles by Hatcher, Clemmer, and D'Andraia raise interesting questions for librarians to consider. Do we have succession plans? Should we have them? How will today's emphasis on the business model move into the not-for-profit arena especially for libraries?

Carole S. Armstrong, MLS
*Assistant Director,
Michigan State University Libraries*

*T*he Academic Library Director: Reflections on a Position in Transition successfully grapples with a critical issue in higher education–the change that is occurring on campuses not only within libraries but the wider realm of information management. Faced with rapidly expanding collections, complex personnel issues, the introduction of new technologies, and ever more restricted budgets, university and college libraries have undergone profound upheaval. *The Academic Library Director* suggests how the character of Library Directors has–within one generation–shifted in response to such changes from the traditional scholar librarian to the manager. Judging by the arguments raised in the *Academic Library Director*, the position may be facing a major shift in emphasis once again. Library directors must rapidly become both managers and leaders. The rapid advance of technology, both within and outside the library, is changing not only the character of libraries themselves, but it is also changing the relationship of libraries to their users and to other campus technology centers. *The Academic Library Director* offers keen insight into the challenges faced by today's library director and should therefore prove to be an invaluable tool for directors, as well as to university administrators who must assess the performance of library directors. It might even prove of value to search committees in their selection of individuals to fill what is an increasingly complex and challenging position.

Clifton H. Jones
Dean, University Libraries
Idaho State University

*T*he Academic Library Director is an outstanding compilation of practical advice and helpful theory and issues review. This is one book that individuals holding these complex and challenging positions can use for up-to-date, insightful information about real issues. Also, busy people will appreciate the clear, high quality, and straightforward writing which speeds the reader along. There is no text wasted. I recommend this publication to present and future library directors–it's well worth your time.

Sarah C. Michalak
Director of the Marriott Library,
University of Utah, Salt Lake City, UT

This unusual collection of papers focuses on aspects of the academic library director position. Paul Kobulnicky's unique piece describes the acting directorship experience and offers suggestions including a modus operandi for those considering accepting an interim position. In her description of her recent survey on the succession paths of directors of middle-sized academic libraries as represented in the Council on State University Libraries, Karen Hatcher presents findings which contrast with previous studies. Joel Clemmer's thoughtful offering compares and contrasts the characteristics of academic directorships at liberal arts colleges with research library positions. One chapter addresses characteristics needed in academic library directors. Another, written by a college dean who served as an interim library director, describes her college's redefinition of the position and subsequent search for a vice provost for information. The final chapter centers on current challenges to higher education and how they affect academic library directors facing the threshold of the 21st century.

This book is a must for any AUL contemplating an acting directorship. I wish I had read it before I interviewed for an interim position . . . or applied for academic director positions. This book should be required reading for provosts embarking on a search for a new academic library director. It is an interesting read for experienced library directors as well.

Marion T. Reid
Dean,
Library & Information Services,
California State University,
San Marcos

The Haworth Press, Inc.

The Academic Library Director: Reflections on a Position in Transition

The Management of Library and Information Studies Education, edited by Herman L. Totten

Vendor Evaluation and Acquisition Budgets, edited by Sul H. Lee

Developing Library Staff for the 21st Century, edited by Maureen Sullivan

Collection Assessment and Acquisitions Budgets, edited by Sul H. Lee

Leadership in Academic Libraries: Proceedings of the W. Porter Kellam Conference, The University of Georgia, May 7, 1991, edited by William Gray Potter

Integrating Total Quality Management in a Library Setting, edited by Susan Jurow and Susan B. Barnard

Catalysts for Change: Managing Libraries in the 1990s, edited by Gisela M. von Dran and Jennifer Cargill

The Role and Future of Special Collections in Research Libraries: British and American Perspectives, edited by Sul H. Lee

Declining Acquisitions Budgets: Allocation, Collection Development and Impact Communication, edited by Sul H. Lee

Libraries as User-Centered Organizations: Imperatives for Organizational Change, edited by Meredith A. Butler

Access, Ownership, and Resource Sharing, edited by Sul H. Lee

The Dynamic Library Organizations in a Changing Environment, edited by Joan Giesecke

The Future of Information Services, edited by Virginia Steel and C. Brigid Welch

The Future of Resource Sharing, edited by Shirley K. Baker and Mary E. Jackson

Libraries and Student Assistants: Critical Links, edited by William K. Black

Managing Change in Academic Libraries, edited by Joseph J. Branin

Access, Resource Sharing, and Collection Development, edited by Sul H. Lee

Interlibrary Loan/Document Delivery and Customer Satisfaction: Strategies for Redesigning Services, edited by Pat L. Weaver-Meyers, Wilbur A. Stolt, and Yem S. Fong

Emerging Patterns of Collection Development in Expanding Resource Sharing, Electronic Information, and Network Environment, edited by Sul H. Lee

The Academic Library Director: Reflections on a Position in Transition, edited by Frank D'Andraia

These books were published simultaneously as special thematic issues of the *Journal of Library Administration* and are available bound separately. For further information, call 1-800-HAWORTH (outside US/Canada: 607-722-5857), Fax 1-800-895-0582 (outside US/Canada: 607-771-0012) or e-mail getinfo@haworth.com

The Academic Library Director: Reflections on a Position in Transition has also been published as *Journal of Library Administration*, Volume 24, Number 3 1997.

The development, preparation, and publication of this work has been undertaken with great care. However, the publisher, employees, editors, and agents of The Haworth Press and all imprints of The Haworth Press, Inc., including The Haworth Medical Press and Pharmaceutical Products Press, are not responsible for any errors contained herein or for consequences that may ensue from use of materials or information contained in this work. Opinions expressed by the author(s) are not necessarily those of The Haworth Press, Inc.

The Haworth Press, Inc., 10 Alice Street, Binghamton, NY 13904-1580 USA

Cover design by Thomas J. Mayshock, Jr.

Library of Congress Cataloging-in-Publication Data

The academic library director : reflections on a position in transition / Frank D'Andraia, editor.
    p. cm.
    Has also been published as Journal of library administration, v. 24, no. 3, 1997"–T.p. verso.
    Includes bibliographical references and index.
    ISBN 0-7890-0320-1 (alk. paper)
    1. Academic libraries–United States–Administration. I. D'Andraia, Frank.
Z675.J5A3388 1997
027.7–dc21
                                                      97-10967
                                                         CIP

The Academic
Library Director:
Reflections on a Position
in Transition

Frank D'Andraia
Editor

The Haworth Press, Inc.
New York · London

INDEXING & ABSTRACTING

Contributions to this publication are selectively indexed or abstracted in print, electronic, online, or CD-ROM version(s) of the reference tools and information services listed below. This list is current as of the copyright date of this publication. See the end of this section for additional notes.

- *Academic Abstracts/CD-ROM,* EBSCO Publishing Editorial Department, P.O. Box 590, Ipswich, MA 01938-0590

- *Academic Search: data base of 2,000 selected academic serials, updated monthly,* EBSCO Publishing, 83 Pine Street, Peabody, MA 01960

- *AGRICOLA Database,* National Agricultural Library, 10301 Baltimore Boulevard, Room 002, Beltsville, MD 20705

- *Cambridge Scientific Abstracts, Health & Safety Science Abstracts,* Environmental Routenet (accessed via INTERNET), 7200 Wisconsin Avenue #601, Bethesda, MD 20814

- *CNPIEC Reference Guide: Chinese National Directory of Foreign Periodicals,* P.O. Box 88, Beijing, People's Republic of China

- *Current Articles on Library Literature and Services (CALLS),* Pakistan Library Association, Quaid-e-Azam Library, Bagh-e-Jinnah, Lahore, Pakistan

- *Current Awareness Abstracts,* Association for Information Management, Information House, 20-24 Old Street, London EC1V 9AP, England

- *Current Index to Journals in Education,* Syracuse University, 4-194 Center for Science and Technology, Syracuse, NY 13244-4100

(continued)

- *Educational Administration Abstracts (EAA),* Sage Publications, Inc., 2455 Teller Road, Newbury Park, CA 91320

- *Higher Education Abstracts,* Claremont Graduate School, 231 East Tenth Street, Claremont, CA 91711

- *IBZ International Bibliography of Periodical Literature,* Zeller Verlag GmbH & Co., P.O.B. 1949, d-49009 Osnabruck, Germany

- *Index to Periodical Articles Related to Law,* University of Texas, 727 East 26th Street, Austin, TX 78705

- *Information Reports & Bibliographies,* Science Associates International, Inc., 6 Hastings Road, Marlboro, NJ 07746-1313

- *Information Science Abstracts,* Plenum Publishing Company, 233 Spring Street, New York, NY 10013-1578

- *Informed Librarian, The,* Infosources Publishing, 140 Norma Road, Teaneck, NJ 07666

- *INSPEC Information Services,* Institution of Electrical Engineers, Michael Faraday House, Six Hills Way, Stevenage, Herts SG1 2AY, England

- *INTERNET ACCESS (& additional networks) Bulletin Board for Libraries ("BUBL"), coverage of information resources on INTERNET, JANET, and other networks.*
  - JANET X.29: UK.AC.BATH.BUBL or 00006012101300
  - TELNET: BUBL.BATH.AC.UK or 138.38.32.45 login 'bubl'
  - Gopher: BUBL.BATH.AC.UK (138.32.32.45). Port 7070
  - World Wide Web: http: / / www.bubl.bath.ac.uk./BUBL/ home.html
  - NISSWAIS: telnetniss.ac.uk (for the NISS gateway)
  The Andersonian Library, Curran Building, 101 St. James Road, Glasgow G4 ONS, Scotland

(continued)

- *Journal of Academic Librarianship: Guide to Professional Literature, The,* Grad School of Library & Information Science/ Simmons College, 300 The Fenway, Boston, MA 02115-5898

- *Konyvtari Figyelo-Library Review,* National Szechenyi Library, Centre for Library and Information Science, H-1827 Budapest, Hungary

- *Library & Information Science Abstracts (LISA),* Bowker-Saur Limited, Maypole House, Maypole Road, East Grinstead, West Sussex RH19 1HH, England

- *Library Literature,* The H.W. Wilson Company, 950 University Avenue, Bronx, NY 10452

- *MasterFILE: updated database from EBSCO Publishing,* 83 Pine Street, Peabody, MA 01960

- *Newsletter of Library and Information Services,* China Sci-Tech Book Review, Library of Academia Sinica, 8 Kexueyuan Nanlu, Zhongguancun, Beijing 100080, People's Republic of China

- *OT BibSys,* American Occupational Therapy Foundation, P.O. Box 31220, Rockville, MD 20824-1220

- *PASCAL International Bibliography T205: Sciences de l'information Documentation,* INIST/CNRS-Service Gestion des Documents Primaries, 2, Allee du Parc de Brabois, F-54514 Vandoeuvre-les-Nancy, Cedex, France

- *Public Affairs Information Bulletin (PAIS),* Public Affairs Information Service, Inc., 521 West 43rd Street, New York, NY 10036-4396

- *Referativnyi Zhurnal (Abstracts Journal of the Institute of Scientific Information of the Republic of Russia),* The Institute of Scientific Information, Baltijskaja ul., 14, Moscow A-219, Republic of Russia

- *Trade & Industry Index,* Information Access Company, 362 Lakeside Drive, Foster City, CA 94404

(continued)

SPECIAL BIBLIOGRAPHIC NOTES

related to special journal issues (separates)
and indexing/abstracting

❏ indexing/abstracting services in this list will also cover material in any "separate" that is co-published simultaneously with Haworth's special thematic journal issue or DocuSerial. Indexing/abstracting usually covers material at the article/chapter level.

❏ monographic co-editions are intended for either non-subscribers or libraries which intend to purchase a second copy for their circulating collections.

❏ monographic co-editions are reported to all jobbers/wholesalers/approval plans. The source journal is listed as the "series" to assist the prevention of duplicate purchasing in the same manner utilized for books-in-series.

❏ to facilitate user/access services all indexing/abstracting services are encouraged to utilize the co-indexing entry note indicated at the bottom of the first page of each article/chapter/contribution.

❏ this is intended to assist a library user of any reference tool (whether print, electronic, online, or CD-ROM) to locate the monographic version if the library has purchased this version but not a subscription to the source journal.

❏ individual articles/chapters in any Haworth publication are also available through the Haworth Document Delivery Services (HDDS).

The Academic Library Director: Reflections on a Position in Transition

CONTENTS

ABOUT THE EDITOR

Frank D'Andraia, MLS, is Director of Libraries at the University of North Dakota, Grand Forks, a position he has held since 1990. Previously, he was Head of Technical Services at the University of California, Riverside. He is an active member of the American Library Association and does writing and presentations on library management. Mr. D'Andraia has served on the editorial board of national library publications; been an advisor and consultant to colleges and bibliographic utilities; been Chair of the Governor's (ND) Advisory Council on Libraries; served as Trustee of the North Dakota Coalition for Adult Literacy; and taught in several library science programs. He is currently serving his second year as Chair and Trustee of The Nature Conservancy of the Dakotas.

Introduction

Frank D'Andraia

In today's "knowledge society," employers have many new expectations for their workers, as well as their managers. Higher education and more specifically, academic libraries and those responsible for administering them, are not immune from these trends.

The articles in this collection focus on many of the issues that face today's academic library director. The authors address the changing nature of work and the new demands placed on library directors. They talk about directors and their credentials and paths to position, including the challenges of being an interim director. They reflect on the perceptions and goals that directors have about their position, as well as collegiate and library culture. Lastly, they talk about the different forces buffeting higher education and their impact on libraries and those who direct them.

The series has been written by individuals associated with colleges and universities from around the nation. The authors have a broad range of educational and professional experience and offer a unique insight on a management position that is truly in transition.

Paul Kobulnicky's article considers the challenges of leading an academic library through the transitional period between permanent directors. His work provides added insight on a subject that is not extensively covered in the literature.

Karen Hatcher writes about career paths for academic library directors. Hatcher's study is based on a survey of 21 academic

[Haworth co-indexing entry note]: "Introduction." D'Andraia, Frank. Co-published simultaneously in the *Journal of Library Administration* (The Haworth Press, Inc.) Vol. 24, No. 3, 1997, pp. 1-2; and: *The Academic Library Director: Reflections on a Position in Transition* (ed: Frank D'Andraia) The Haworth Press, Inc., 1997, pp. 1-2. Single or multiple copies of this article are available for a fee from The Haworth Document Delivery Service [1-800-342-9678, 9:00 a.m. - 5:00 p.m. (EST). E-mail address: getinfo@ haworth.com].

1

library directors associated with institutions who are members of the Council of State University Libraries (COSUL).

Rebecca Martin explores the many changes affecting higher education and the impact these changes are having on the evolving position of academic library director. She identifies criteria that will be valuable to those involved in recruiting academic library leaders for the 21st century.

Barbara Brittingham reflects on how the University of Rhode Island conducted its search for a newly configured position of Vice Provost for Information and Dean of University Libraries. Brittingham provides a unique perspective, for her observations are made from the point of view of a non-librarian.

Joel Clemmer surveyed a select number of "Oberlin Group" library directors who recently assumed college library directorships after having worked in university library settings. Clemmer discusses the perceptions these directors have about collegiate life vis-à-vis the realities since assuming their responsibilities.

Frank D'Andraia concludes with a chapter on the challenges that face academic library directors as the library business migrates toward adopting a more businesslike model.

In closing, I wish to thank several people whose assistance was greatly appreciated. They are as follows: Ms. Karen Cloud and Dr. Janet Spaeth of the University of North Dakota, Grand Forks; Dr. Joan Giesecke of the University of Nebraska, Lincoln; Tom Leonhardt of the University of Oklahoma, Norman; and Dr. Gloria Cline of the University of Southwestern Louisiana, Lafayette.

Between the Acts:
The Interim or Acting Director
of a Research Library

Paul J. Kobulnicky

INTRODUCTION

The most important issue in libraries for the past two decades has been the management of change. Technological, economic and social factors have forced librarians to question the professional foundations that have been the basis for traditional services and to develop and implement new services that hold promise to be more appropriate for the future. The movement from the past to the future, however, goes through the present. Choices must be made daily, not only about which elements of the past we abandon or retain but also about the extent and timing of new initiatives. In many cases we choose to maintain expensive duplicative services to provide a stable transition from the past into the future. Without experience to guide us, decisions about abandoning past services too quickly or instituting future services before their time are risky. Not only are there many possible choices for future services but all too often the need to build technologically sophisticated, and thus expensive, information delivery infrastructures makes those choices

Paul J. Kobulnicky is Director of Libraries, University of Connecticut, Storrs, CT (e-mail: knicky@unconnvm.uconn.edu).

[Haworth co-indexing entry note]: "Between the Acts: The Interim or Acting Director of a Research Library." Kobulnicky, Paul J. Co-published simultaneously in the *Journal of Library Administration* (The Haworth Press, Inc.) Vol. 24, No. 3, 1997, pp. 3-29; and: *The Academic Library Director: Reflections on a Position in Transition* (ed: Frank D'Andraia) The Haworth Press, Inc., 1997, pp. 3-29. Single or multiple copies of this article are available for a fee from The Haworth Document Delivery Service [1-800-342-9678, 9:00 a.m. - 5:00 p.m. (EST). E-mail address: getinfo@haworth.com].

3

even riskier. Financial resources are declining both in real and apparent terms. Staff sizes are declining and remaining library staff are increasingly strained to do all that must be done. Critical beyond all other factors, however, is the very high rate of change. The lifetime of a new service, instituted today, is most likely measured in months. In years past, librarians typically worked for the better part of a year to set a new process into place with the anticipated yield of many years of predictable work flowing through that process. Today, the very implementation of a new process signals the beginning of the next revision. The rate of change currently being experienced by libraries has increased the importance of effective leadership. In order for the staff to successfully respond to these rates of change, they must feel that the other portions of their work environment are as stable as possible. The staff must be able to rely on leadership, especially the director, to help them manage change by focusing the collective actions of the organization and by minimizing chaos. The library director must build, with the staff, an effective vision for the future and then guide the library toward that vision. Such environmental stability is the responsibility of the director. If the director's position itself lacks stability then there is a great potential for the entire staff to respond negatively and for the organization's services to suffer.

Obviously, directors are not permanent. Each year directors retire, change institutions or, for other reasons, leave their positions.[1] In the period between permanent directors, someone must be designated to lead the organization. The search for a new library director involves a protracted process that is very common in higher education. It is traditional that everyone with an academic or administrative position is hired only after a full national search has been completed.[2] Even when undertaken with the best intentions for swiftness, search processes are seldom completed in less than three months and most often the process takes six to nine months. In the time frame of turbulent change, six months is now a very long period of time for an organization to be without stable leadership.

This article considers the challenge of leading an organization through the transitional period for libraries when they are between permanent directors. Much of my own interest in this issue and my awareness of the challenges inherent in the "interim" director position come from my own four year assignment as the Interim Director[3] at a major research library. With the notable exception of Euster and Solomon,[4] little has been written about the "acting" or "interim" director in libraries, nor about other "acting" positions such as college or university presidents, provosts or deans. In order to more accurately discuss the issues involved in leading a contemporary research library on an "acting" or "interim" basis, 15 other individuals who have served in that capacity were interviewed.[5] In addition to providing valuable insight on an assignment that each interviewee reported to be a very difficult time in his or her professional career,[6] the interviews also provided insight into more general themes of research library management.

> The culture of the academic library is resistant to authority of any kind. Even in the best of circumstances, acting directors must be assertive in order to exercise the limited authority of that position.

This is the easiest job I have had since 1979.

Although the issues of establishing leadership that face the new acting director are fundamentally the same issues that face any new permanent director, the circumstances of being "acting" make this a distinctly different challenge. Leadership is certainly required of the acting director but, when compared to a permanent director, leadership is much more difficult to achieve. The acting director has neither the permanent director's validation and mandate from the search nor the independence that comes from being new to the organization. Leadership must be established very quickly, often damaging perceptions of the "due process," to move effectively through the potentially short interim period. No matter how long the interim period is proposed to be, the staff recognizes that new (different) permanent leadership will eventually arrive. The inherently limited tenure of the acting director gives those who disagree with the organization's interim directions reason to "wait it out." Most importantly, the acting director is normally hesitant to undertake major change that might be counter to a new permanent director's objectives.

Being the acting director was fun but being the director was a lot more fun.

The interviews were conducted by telephone during the period August-October 1995. Each interview lasted approximately one hour. Those interviewed included library directors, assistant/associate directors and academic faculty who had served, or were then serving, in an "interim" capacity. They were given a set of questions before the interview to help them to organize their thoughts, but the actual responses sought were their most intense observations and recollections. The responses that did come back were as varied as the specific situations that each individual experienced but there were many common threads that defined the sense of difficulty inherent in the "interim" position. Each person was asked to consider four distinct periods in their "interim" experience: the events up to the time full authority was passed to them, the subsequent "acting" period until the search for a permanent director was formally underway, the period during the search and the period after the search. Each of these broad periods focuses upon a different set of the challenges associated with the "interim" director role.

The issues addressed in this article will be divided into two sections. The first will deal with the problems associated with the "acting director" position, both for the person serving as the acting director and for the organization. The second section will focus on a set of recommendations for a successful interim period.

THE CHALLENGES OF "ACTING" DIRECTORSHIPS

Carrying out the assignment of the acting director is difficult because the assignment's only single common objective is to successfully bring itself to a conclusion. This is to be contrasted with the permanent director whose objective is to lead the organization toward the completion of tangible organizational and service goals. The time available to solidify leadership and to refocus the organization on service objectives is short. The limited time scale of the acting directorship is further divided into four distinct periods: the period when the acting director is chosen and agrees to serve, the early acting directorship, the active period of the search for the permanent director, and the period after the search has been completed. These periods further constrict the possibilities of the acting director for the accomplishment of service-related objectives and each has its own particular challenges.

The Choice of the Acting Director

> No provost[7] understands libraries. They know that it [the library] is a sensitive issue on campus and that it can blow up on them.

Libraries, especially academic libraries, have very little in common with the military or even with commerce when it comes to the concept of "next in command." The culture of the academe promotes egalitarianism and collegiality. It is seldom that we mentor, train or otherwise prepare librarians to be ready to take up the leadership role at the exact moment that the need arises. Traditional library organizational structures with an administrative council reporting to the director do not identify, either internally or externally, a formal succession of command.[8] Thus, the most often asked question following an announcement, or more likely a rumor, that the current director will step down is, "Who will be 'acting?'" From this scenario, a number of issues presage the difficult period that is to follow.

One of the first issues is who knows what and when do they know it. Many of those interviewed spoke of being aware that their name was being put forward for the position long before they were actually and officially approached. A few even reported that the entire library staff was consulted on who the interim director ought to be and thus the discussion was somewhat open. More commonly, however, the unofficial message was often conveyed by the departing director, a member of the provost's staff, a member of the search committee or by an individual out of the administrative stream who happened to be the confidant of someone highly placed. One of the first stresses felt by the future acting director, and too often a harbinger of things to come is the wait, with the associated anxiety and self doubt, for the call from the provost to actually discuss the opportunity. When the call to meet and discuss the opportunity comes it is seldom unexpected. The conversation with the provost is the next challenge to be met.

> You don't realize how much you can negotiate just because the institution wants stability.

Candidates for the acting directorship usually have little negotiating experience. It has been my observation that librarians operate with a very high degree of institutional loyalty. When an individual is asked to take up the leadership mantle for the good of the organization they usually have one or more of the following responses: they are good soldiers and their loyalty will not permit them to do anything but that which is asked of them; they are the only logical choice based upon factors of position, seniority or previous enterprise-wide assignments and thus it is their contracted duty; or they are flattered and honored to have been chosen. Whatever the reason or set of reasons, they are seldom prepared or mentored to negotiate from a position of strength. They do not fully recognize their complete set of options or their personal liabilities. To be chosen to be the acting director in the first place makes ample case in the mind of the provost that the candidate is savvy enough to effectively negotiate personal and corporate conditions for acceptance.

There are a number of issues that are often overlooked by the candidates in the stress of that initial interview. The most important set of issues, as in any management setting, revolves around resources. First and foremost is the magnitude of the job, its enormous workload and the effect that workload will have on the candidate's personal life. This is particularly true if there is a partner, a spouse and/or children involved. Professionally, the candidate does not often think about the cost of replacing him or herself. Often one unrealistically thinks that one can simultaneously continue to do one's old job. In a similar vein, this may also be an opportunity to negotiate for additional human or fiscal resources to undertake a long sought-after project. There are other issues to be negotiated that are not as directly involved with resources.

> You need to minimize the acting period in order to be effective. The longer it drags on the more the staff begin to react out of concern for their long term future.

It is rare indeed that the provost will have thought through or even considered the details of the candidate's personal future or assignment. It is assumed that the candidates will take care of themselves. Here the "acting dean" model is a culprit. The provost subconsciously assumes that tenure is in effect and that the individual can, and perhaps wants to, return to the faculty role. The provost does not think to discuss ways to minimize the duration of the interim period nor often cares that it is minimized since salary savings may be in effect. The salary savings issue is especially valid if the resource negotiations mentioned above were not undertaken. The provost may also be less than eager to raise the issue of the interim director's ability to be a candidate for the director position.

> The longer your period of acting the worse your chance at being the director.

The issue of the acting director's ability to be a candidate for the permanent directorship is one that is difficult for the provost to address. The provost needs an emotionally strong and confident individual to lead the library during the interim period. Thus, the acting director candidate must be assured that he or she is in a strong position to be a candidate for the permanent directorship. In addition, to be in compliance with the policies for searches, the provost must, if asked, state that the search is open to anyone. However, the institution and/or the provost may have a very definite desire to seek someone from outside the present staff to be the permanent director. The astute negotiator will know to raise this issue and interpret the responses, often by stating an unwillingness to be an active candidate. The qualities to be sought in a new director are often related to the views of the membership of the coming search committee. At the time of the negotiations, the provost has not likely thought about the search committee, its leadership, membership or the involvement of the library staff in the search process. These issues are all points that can be negotiated as can the interim assignment.

> The university administration does not know what they do want but, they do know that they don't want anything bad to happen.

> Provost to interim director: "On library matters, I think what you think."

The provost has likely not given much thought to any detailed assignment for the interim period except the obvious, visible, public and/or nagging problems typically associated with costs, faculty-library relations and, in a few cases, student-library relations. This can be an opportunity for the astute candidate to raise interim goals such as "organizational healing versus the initiation of rapid change," the evaluation of library programs by external consultants, library staff input to the provost on the qualities of the next director, shifts in the ownership/access ratio in collections, information technology investments and service changes. It is seldom that the provost will raise such issues as many of them are viewed as the charge of the next director. The fundamental goal of the provost is to get the basic issue of who temporarily runs the library off of his or her agenda as soon as possible so as to move on to other problems. That urgency is the leverage for negotiation that the more naive candidate all too often misses. Once past, it cannot be recovered.

The Interim Period

> Once you are in place, make clear your charge to the rest of the library faculty and staff so they have clear expectations of how you are approaching the acting role.

Many of those interviewed described how excited they were to get started and how full of energy they felt. Most acting directors were previously well-placed in the organization and being appointed acting director was the perfect challenge. It required them to stretch to their maximum abilities but it was a reasonable stretch. Thus, at the very beginning of the interim period and with the reality of the search for the new director as far off as it will be, the acting director can undertake to exert leadership within the organization while the organization's attention is focused on success during the interim rather than on the coming of a new director. The staff wants to see what the acting director will do to address past problems, to take advantage of opportunities or to help the organization position itself for, and in some cases before, the next director. The first weeks and months of the acting director's tenure are marked by high organizational energy, cooperation and good will. This is not to say that these days are without problems for the acting director.

Starting to change a poor culture is very difficult.

During the early days of the interim period, the sense of well being in the organization is largely dependent upon the conditions within the organization when the acting director was appointed. In general, organizational cultures are difficult to change. Thus, staff within a culture that had become defensive, mistrustful or otherwise inwardly focused will need to be led through a healing process before they can be led to more externally focused endeavors. This requires greater attention to "process" than to outcomes. It is extremely important for the new acting director to join with others in the organization in seeking consensus about actions that should be undertaken in the interim period. Such a process thus develops an agenda that is not as much a statement about the acting director as it is about the success of the organization. On the other hand, an organization whose culture was healthy and more externally focused, while still concerned with due process, will be more concerned with demonstrating that it can maintain a high level of achievement. Successful leadership during the interim period is often a matter of recognizing the needs of the organization for healing versus action.

Gauge your culture. Are you already first among equals?

The acting director's former position in the organization is also a significant factor in his or her early success. The transition is usually smooth and early success is likely if the incumbent is viewed by the staff as the most properly placed individual in the organizational hierarchy to assume a leadership role. Individuals with the title of "deputy director" are good examples of properly placed individuals. Other logical individuals are associate directors. However, the choice among associate directors can be contentious, especially if there have previously been struggles among those individuals for influence within the organization or if more than one individual might want to be a candidate for the permanent directorship. Where there is, or was, contention, a candidate for acting director who has seniority or who has organization-wide, rather than line, responsibility can help to make the choice more broadly consensual. The objective is to identify an individual whose choice, in a time of organizational upheaval, does not raise more problems than it solves.

> A faculty member who served as an acting director: "The deans have each other. The library director is the loneliest job in the university."

At times individuals are chosen outside the expected library hierarchy. Either a member of the library staff is chosen who is lower in the organizational chart by managerial level or by seniority than a more logical choice or someone from outside the library staff is chosen. Individuals chosen from outside the library staff have been faculty, library school faculty or university administrators of all types. Such action usually occurs when the provost either lacks confidence in those who are in the logical positions or when a more "neutral" individual is sought. In either case, any non-traditionally placed individual who accepts such a role must spend most of his or her early period building trust and forging relationships. Although such an appointment may be necessary, it is a very difficult move for the well being of the library and the library staff. In addition, the provost must be willing to give time and energy to be visibly, vocally and continually supportive of that candidate.

> It is critical to avoid the appearance of floundering.

> You may be merely an "acting" director but others are watching to see how the system responds to a new hand on the tiller.

No matter what the previous role, early success for the acting director is also a matter of recognizing that there are two constituencies that must be served, the internal and the external. Much has already been noted about the importance of the acting director's responding to the needs of the internal (library staff) and responding accordingly. However, it is the director who has the primary role of external relations and these relations cannot be abandoned during the interim period.

> In order to be plugged in to what is going on on our campuses, we have to identify with the academic administrators.

The acting director must assure deans, faculty and student groups that the library continues to have firm and responsive leadership and that it is acting in the best interest of the university. The acting director must also make sure that library friends, donors and foundation directors are made aware of the plans for the interim period and for the search to follow. Relations with external constituents can be one of the most difficult responsibilities for the acting director since it is the one area in which he or she is unlikely to have had significant prior experience and where the direct and personal involvement of the former director may have been the most critical factor of success.

> Being an acting director was a powerful experience for me. It is a wonderful opportunity for gaining insight about library administration no matter what the aspirations of the actor.

There is, in fact, no experience quite like being a director of libraries. Much of the early success of the acting director is dependent upon a realization that he or she is now the director. This is largely a realization that one is in a new and much larger role. Actions that were once an integral part of the way in which the candidate performed his or her former job may now be viewed as inappropriate for someone who is the acting director. Where once it was important to be seen as a colleague, now the acting director must be seen as a leader. Where the individual may have once proposed many ideas for discussion, the director must now focus the organization. Former relationships with colleagues may be strained as the acting director seeks distance from old relationships to ensure the perception of objectivity. The priority of the acting director must be on the health and success of the entire organization rather than on the maintenance of former relationships. For the new acting director, one of the most difficult habits to change is that of appropriate talk.

We talk to each other way too much.

I was a lot less plugged in than I used to be.

When you have not been a director or held a similar leadership role, it is difficult to fathom how much importance is given to what the director says. There is an understandable tendency to always try to convince your colleagues or explain your actions when the position demands the more subtle roles of education and articulation of decisions. It is crucial to the early success of the acting director to recognize that listening is more important than speaking, questioning more important than stating, and the maintenance of silence more important that idle chatter. Most of all, it is important to remember that what the acting director says will be remembered, even when the acting director never intended it to be remembered. There is a difference in perspective between the acting director and the staff. The acting director continues to strive for collegiality while the staff sees the acting director become (consciously or unconsciously) a very significant, and potentially controlling, figure in their personal and professional lives. This difference has the potential to lead to many misunderstandings. When these perspectives are combined with the inherent weaknesses of the acting director position and the potential for some staff to reject that individual's leadership, the acting director must always respond cautiously.

Mind your temper for you will be provoked.

The Search . . . Things Change

Once the search starts, people in the library seem to decompensate and get testy about small grievances–change does not come without its threats–and the acting director must perform as a steady calming influence who is quasi-parental. (Eric Solomon in Euster and Solomon[9])

You might as well be a window. Everyone looks right through you. Distraction is everywhere. Talk is about candidates but you're not involved.

Once the search begins, the period of excitement for the acting director usually ends. The search process itself begins to be the primary attention of the library staff and of the library's principal constituents. Everyone concentrates on the future leadership of the library and the associated decisions leading to that new leadership. Much of the early discussion is on the question of who is to be on the search committee and who is to chair it. For the acting director, an effort must be made to gain the library staff's adequate representation on the search committee. Once the search committee is selected, the focus shifts to the construction of the advertisement and the list of qualities that the university uses to describe what it seeks in new leadership. This is the first of many instances where the acting director can begin to evaluate his or her potential candidacy against some public criteria. It can also be the first indication that the organization is articulating goals and needs that are divergent from the acting director's strengths, and even actions, during the interim period.

> Being a candidate brought out support I didn't know was there. Nothing can take that away.

Here, in fact, two roads begin to diverge. If the acting director is determined not to be a candidate, then a role as a caretaker begins to take shape even if the acting director was an activist leader before the search. The acting director's responsibilities now are to assist in the search process, counsel and calm the staff and begin to prepare for the eventual change. If the search process should eventually fail, then the role of the acting director must be re-evaluated. More will be said about this eventuality later. However, if the acting director expects to be a candidate, then his or her role in and during the search process becomes much more complex. At this point, every past and present action of the acting director has potential to lose much of its objective value and become fodder for debate about motives and intentions. To counter this potentiality, the library's goals and the associated actions of the acting director who is a candidate for the directorship must have been formed by organizational consensus early in the acting director's tenure. Further, such consensus must be constantly communicated to the staff during the interim period if the staff are to comfortably move forward toward their goals during the disruption occasioned by the search.

One of the most difficult periods for the acting director who is a candidate is the time when other candidates are on campus. It is very hard for most acting directors to see the staff focusing their attention on other candidates when they themselves have been working to provide the leadership for which the other candidates can only offer promise. The question of whether it is proper for the acting director/candidate to meet with the other candidates to appraise them of local issues and to answer necessary questions often seems to search committees to be improper and unequal. However, when the acting director is removed from the search process he or she is also kept at a distance from the concerns of the rest of the staff and isolated from the very system he or she is charged to lead. Information about the search often flows to the most junior member of the library staff before it flows to the acting director. The maneuvers that are taken by members of the search committee and the library staff to keep from giving the appearance of a conflict of interest often seem, especially to the acting director, absurd. In addition, the actions of the search committee to maintain rigorous adherence to process often discount the committee's potential adverse effect on the internal candidate's professional reputation. Such is the price that the acting director pays to be a candidate for the directorship. Sooner or later, the choice is made.

The Aftermath

> Why can't the end of the search go through with dignity . . . with concern for the internal candidates? Why does it, the search process, have to be so pure?

For the acting director who was not a candidate, the successfully completed search for a new director begins an inevitable progress toward transition. One of the first items on the new director's agenda will be to establish both short and long term relationships for the acting director. Typically, in the short term the acting director becomes an agent for the new director, facilitating communications, moving forward or holding on issues and helping with the logistical arrangements for the coming of the director. Often this short term arrangement carries over to operational control of the library while the new director spends the first weeks on campus meeting with the staff and major constituents. A longer term relationship usually evolves during the first several months of the new director's tenure. Long term relationships usually are one of three possibilities. The former acting director may return to his or her former position in the organization; the former acting director is recognized for the leadership skills he or she has gained and is given the clear number two position in the organization; or the former acting director recognizes that it is time for him or her to move on to seek another position outside the library system he or she has just led . . . perhaps a directorship. However, these choices have greater potential for the non-candidate.

Although there are numerous examples of individuals who have been acting directors and who have stayed on in their organizations in capacities below the directorship after failing as a candidate for the directorship, such situations present greater challenges for both the acting director and the new director. It is the exceptional director who can make a former leader of the organization an effective subordinate. It requires the new director to truly value the work of the acting director and to incorporate it into the new director's vision. It is also difficult for the acting director to put aside feelings of rejection and the anger that goes with that rejection and to subordinate his or her vision and intimate knowledge of the staff to the vision and aspirations of the new director. Success in such situations has, understandably, an inverse relationship to the length of the acting director's tenure as an acting director. The longer the tenure, the more ownership the acting director feels in his or her programs and visions. Success is also more likely if the acting director was formerly the clear number two person in the organization and will return to that number two position. For many acting directors, whether they were candidates or not, the experience is so powerful that they naturally move on to lead another organization.

One of the most contentious issues for both search committees and acting directors who are candidates is how far does the institution move the acting director's candidacy forward because they are a "local" candidate. The perspective of most search committees is that each candidate, internal or external, must be evaluated with the same objective criteria. The perspective of most internal candidates is that they should be afforded every possible benefit by the search committee in recognition of their knowledge of the local issues and their service to the institution. The acting director as candidate has one additional perspective. He or she has moved into the highest and most visible levels of the profession with personal risk associated with the difficulties of the acting directorship. Each hopes, at the very least, to move as far forward as possible in the search so as to be well-positioned for other director searches. The perspectives of internal candidates and of search committees are seldom similar.

RECOMMENDATIONS FOR SUCCESS

Based on their experiences, the individuals interviewed were asked what they would recommend that future acting directors do in order to maximize the experience for themselves and for their organization. It should be noted that the recommendations are much more germane for an acting director who envisions an interim period of more than several months. Where the interim period is certain to be only a matter of two or three months, the best, and only, advice is to be a patient and calm steward of the organization until the next director arrives. Where the interim period is indefinite or longer than several months, the recommendations are important.

Seek Advice

I thought I was well prepared until the first week on the job.

I was not well prepared for the politics . . . not well prepared for the isolation.

There have been many individuals who have had the experience of being an acting director of a research library. There is a great similarity to their experiences and their reactions to those experiences. Potential candidates should make efforts early on to seek the advice of those who have had such experiences. Past directors of the library are the first and most obvious stop. Through personal contacts, the candidate can discuss the particular situation that one is being asked to undertake and can get detailed advice on how to negotiate and proceed. As in any other data gathering exercise, the more advice that one gets from different sources, the more likely it is that a good plan of action can be crafted. Getting advice early on in the process can not only help to avoid costly mistakes but can provide the candidate with a set of future mentors and supporters.

Negotiate Well in the Beginning

Recognize that the larger institution, as represented by the provost, is fundamentally interested in maximizing stability and minimizing problems. The provost usually wants to get to the successful completion of a search for a new director without having to be aware that there even was an interim period. This means that there are only two points when the provost will be fully engaged in the process, at the very beginning and at the very end. Many of those interviewed mentioned the importance of negotiations with the provost at the opening stages. The provost has the immediate problem of finding interim leadership and will give up resources to secure that leadership. Once interim leadership is secured, resources from the provost are very much more difficult to acquire. Those interviewed mentioned several points that are important to build into negotiations.

> Get an understanding of your assignment. Is it more important for the organization to heal and settle or to move forward and change?

The candidate for the acting directorship must negotiate his or her own interests. It is important to secure a full director's salary. The burdens on the acting director and his or her family are significant and one of the only compensations for those burdens is financial remuneration. It is also important to negotiate a clear time frame for the interim period. It is wise to have the period stated contractually. In general, a short period is preferable as it requires the provost to move actively forward on the search and also because short interim periods are generally more successful for both the individual and the organization. However, in some cases, a long interim period is desired by both the candidate and the provost in order to provide time to address serious organizational issues. Long interim periods should definitely be stated contractually so as to provide the candidate with protection from midstream changes of the incumbent in the provost's position or from other organizational or political pressures. The candidate should also get a commitment to regular meetings with the provost or a well-placed member of the provost's staff during the interim period. Finally, it is important to negotiate human resources to cover the acting director's former responsibilities. Here it is wise for the candidate to enter the discussion with a detailed plan, including budget, for covering those responsibilities.

> Outline a short term plan for the University administration and seek their backing for the actions that you expect to be necessary.

On the organizational side, this is an opportunity to gain short term resources to accomplish objectives to move the organization forward. The specific objectives vary with the local scene but they can be acquisitions funds, automation funds, one-time staff funding to accomplish a strategic initiative or funds for a physical renovation or another capital objective. The candidate can indicate that one is only willing to be the interim director if one can be successful (where success is measured by the organization's success) and to be successful in an interim position requires additional resources. Another important negotiating point at some institutions is the ability to affect the formation of the search committee. A number of those interviewed stated that the library staff would not have been included on the search committee for the new director if the acting director had not made it a condition for accepting the acting director position. Such a negotiating tactic not only improves the search process but also raises the image of the acting director among the library staff.

Consider the Staff

> Acknowledge the staff and their accomplishments quickly upon appointment (but only if you can do it genuinely—staff can smell insincerity quickly and your credibility will diminish). A change in management can bring out some insecurity

in some individuals or groups. Reassure them that you know that they are important.

Leadership comes from the willingness of the led to be led. It is critical to recognize the concerns of the staff and to acknowledge their part in the past and future successes of the organization. This is necessary early and often. The staff want to know that they are respected and that there will be a continued tone of respect. In the first days, they should also be told all of the details of the appointment, including the term and the assignments. If a poor organizational climate exists within the library, then this is the opportunity for the acting director to set a tone for the organizational climate that will be expected. Such a new climate should reflect an agreement to, and the enforcement of, basic human values. Inter-organizational communications should be reviewed and enhanced.

Have a Cause

> I suggest that you find a purpose for being the "acting director" from "make this library a saner place to work" to "bring about world peace." Any purpose can work; I suggest that you just have one. When it comes time to make a decision, it is easier to make that decision; i.e., which decision will make this a saner place to work?

Alec Guinness' character Colonel Nicholson forced his troop's attention on the completion of a bridge over the river Kwai in order to keep them functional as a military unit while they were being held captive in the jungles of Burma. In the case of the acting library director, a clearly stated short term objective focuses the organization on that objective instead of the interim status of the director. If the acting director takes this opportunity to state a single purpose for his or her candidacy, then not only are the staff's actions organized around a goal but the decisions of the acting director can be consistently made by asking how it furthers progress toward completion of the goal. The goal becomes a cause. Such short term goals can be as pragmatic as finishing the retrospective conversion of the bibliographic records, clearing up a processing backlog or installing a robust local area network in the entire library. These goals can also be as philosophical as making significant improvements in customer responsiveness, having a library meet one-on-one with each faculty member in the institution or just making the library a more humane place to work. Whatever the goal, it must be stated publicly and often and its symbolic value as a unifying theme should not be understated. If the acting director cannot, through the force of individual character, unify the staff around a cause then other methods must be utilized.

Build Consensus

> Don't try to do it alone and don't step out of character just to assume a role.

> Focus on the positive. Realize that you are responsible. Realize that you are not the only one responsible.

Probably the most frequently stated recommendation by those interviewed was the need for the acting director to seek consensus within the library on an agenda for the interim period. If there is an existing plan, review the plan and reaffirm consensus and commitment to the next objectives within the likely time frame of the interim period. If there is no existing plan, then a short term planning process should be undertaken to identify and gain consensus on goals for the organization during the interim period. In this manner, the acting director facilitates the will of the staff and then manages the implementation of the projects leading to completion of the goals. Depending upon the specific organization and its structure, consensus might be needed among the entire library staff or only among the senior management staff. By building consensus for the goals of the interim period, the acting director not only builds commitment for an action oriented agenda but also avoids unnecessary speculation on the motivation for decisions that are subsequently made with respect to the acting director's candidacy for the directorship.

Consider Cautiously One's Candidacy for the Directorship

> Secure your option to be a candidate at the beginning but do not declare or decide at the outset whether or not you will

apply. The true "interim director"; i.e., the acting director with no prospect of becoming director, has extremely weak authority to lead the library, even temporarily.

Be aware of the limitations on a non-candidate interim director or lame duck.

If the interim period is not fixed in time and no new director has been chosen, then the acting director will have to face the question of whether to be a candidate for the directorship. The decision to be a candidate for the director is the most difficult and political decision that the acting director must make. It is difficult because for many individuals it means crossing an organizational line from which it might be impossible to successfully retreat. Declaring one's intention to be the leader makes it hard, and in some situations impossible, to return to a more collegial position in the organization. It means, therefore, that to be a candidate and then to fail to win the position may imply that the acting director must be prepared to move to a different institution. Often, physical relocation may be impossible because of personal or family considerations. Thus, one of the first things that an acting director should consider when accepting the acting directorship is whether physically moving to a different institution/city/state is a valid option.

The decision to be a candidate is also difficult because the decision is most often possible only after the acting director has had enough time and experience to evaluate his or her own performance and also enough time for others (colleagues, administrators, faculty, etc.) to have observed the acting director and to be able to offer realistic performance indicators. Experience as the acting director also gives the candidate a sense of the job's appeal. Few acting directors fail to rise to the challenge and fail to enjoy the challenge. However, most acting directors do not recognize that opinion until forced by the exigency of an application deadline to make a decision on their candidacy. The generalization is obvious. The more experience one gains, the more effectively one's final decision can be made. However, the longer one waits to declare, the more politically charged the decision becomes and the more stressful it is on the staff.

It is not a good thing for a young, promising individual to be an acting director. It is too risky for his or her career.

There was no consensus among those whom I interviewed on the desirability of the acting director being a candidate for the directorship. Everyone did acknowledge the difficult political aspects of the acting director's candidacy. Acting directors have a history within the organization and that history, for the entire staff, may not be entirely positive. This is especially true for those individuals who either moved up through the ranks, were risk takers, or who pushed aggressive agendas. This is to be contrasted with external candidates who are known largely by reputation of successes or through their resumes. This comparison is especially true if the search committee has no, or minimal, librarian participation to focus the discussions on the significance of the candidate's professional achievements.

The difficult question of whether to be a candidate and the political aspects of that decision are initially a question of timing. As previously mentioned, it is easier to make a good decision on one's candidacy the longer one waits. However, political intrigue among the staff builds as time goes on and that intrigue not only affects staff morale and thus operational efficiency but also affects the acting director's decision to be a candidate. Until the acting director declares or refuses candidacy, the staff spend increasing time speculating, not only on the candidacy, but also on the motivations for operational choices that have been made. The question too often asked is, "Was that a policy or program that was instituted for the good of the organization or to enhance the acting director's candidacy?" As long as the acting director is unannounced as a candidate or announced to be a candidate, such speculation will exist in the organization and will often be detrimental to staff morale and to the candidate.

Not being a candidate made it easier to be an acting director.

I had no desire to be a candidate. No one was trying to make me look bad so that I wouldn't get the job.

From among the varying points of view of those interviewed, I was able to construct one potential strategy for the acting director who wishes to be a director. It is a three-step strategy. The first step is to negotiate beforehand a fixed length contract as acting director and also a leave with pay to follow the end of that contract. One year is a good length for that contract and a six-month leave is sufficient. The second step is to publicly declare, from the very onset of the acting directorship, unequivocally not to be a candidate for the directorship. The third step is to prepare to move to a directorship at another institution during the leave period. This strategy permits the greatest success in the acting role because it promotes the perception that the acting director is working only in the institution's best interest. It permits a clear transition between directors. It also permits the acting director to be a strong, experienced candidate elsewhere. However, this strategy requires vigorous interim leadership to avoid a protracted "lame duck" effect as well as very careful planning and a commitment to a very definitive future.

Since this strategy is rather pure in its concept, variations are most likely. Variations, however, eventually lead to a common thread. If the acting director eventually intends to be a candidate, or is pressured by the administration to be a candidate, then one must begin one's acting period exactly as though one were an experienced director, with a clear vision and a leadership style that exemplifies one's values. There can be no learning period.

TWO OTHER OPTIONS

Non-Librarian Library Directors

There have been many examples of individuals being asked to become the acting director specifically because they are not librarians. This is most often undertaken by the University administration for two reasons. The first is that no librarians are deemed capable of the job or, often, several librarians are potentially so capable, and equal, that they all would be expected to be potential candidates for the directorship and to select one to be acting director would give that individual an unfair advantage. The second reason is that there is a general degree of dissatisfaction with the library as expressed to the administration by the faculty and the interim period is seen as an opportunity to get unbiased information by inserting a relative newcomer into the operation at the highest level.

Individuals considered for acting directorships outside the library staff fall into three categories. If the institution has a school of library science, often a faculty member or administrator from the library school will, because of their subject background, be asked to take on the role. A second category, because of their administrative experience, are deans, assistant/associate deans and members of the provost's staff. Finally, and usually because of a specific interest in the library, faculty members are chosen. Faculty members are often chosen when they have had some previous, formal involvement with the library, typically as the chairperson of the faculty library committee. In general, these appointments work well when two conditions apply. The acting director recognizes and pursues his or her specific skills which may include such areas as educational management, information technology, human relations or simply the traditional scholar's interest in the library. The library staff, in turn, must be supportive and able to run the more detailed or library-professional aspects of the operation.

> A faculty acting director: "I knew how to manage an academic department and how to obtain funds but I didn't know how to manage the technical aspects of the library and I didn't try. I trusted the library administrative staff to do those things."

A growing option is the use of former research library directors to fill the role of acting director. Several ARL directors have stayed on longer than their intended retirement to permit their institutions to re-advertise searches. Other recent ARL directors have advertised their availability as library consultants. Although none of these individuals have yet been hired as acting directors at libraries other than those they formerly directed, the possibility exists and only awaits the right case where experienced leadership is needed, the local staff cannot be tapped for leadership and the price is right. As more research library directors seek early retirement or a more non-traditional end to their careers,[10] this option will become more popular.

CONCLUSION

The acting directorship of a major research library is a critical period in both the life of the organization and the acting director.

Managing change in libraries is difficult under normal circumstances but very difficult with only temporary leadership. Organization distractions, due to interest and intrigue over the selection of the acting director and also the permanent director, are rampant. The interim period typically starts abruptly, has few definitive operation objectives other than organization stability and is politically charged over the opportunity for change. The eventual search for a new director makes the organization lose its focus on operations and thus difficult to administer. Finally, for both the acting director and the staff, the resolution of the search brings the interim period to an end but sets in motion the next set of changes in leadership and organizational initiatives.

During this period, acting directors must not only lead their organizations but they must protect their own professional careers. Negotiations leading to the acting director appointment are critical and can significantly affect the success of acting directorship. Acting directors' careers are vulnerable because they must lead effectively without the imprimatur of the full title of director. Leadership of the organization during this period is most effective if it is not associated with the acting director's candidacy for the directorship, but a long term "lame duck" leadership must be guarded against. The acting directorship is difficult to manage without stress to the actor and to the system but it is an excellent vehicle for rapidly developing and honing an individual's leadership skills.

NOTES

1. As an example of the rate of change, as of 1/96, 24 of the 119 ARL libraries were somewhere in the process of changing leadership.

2. It is interesting to note that for the very reason of the importance of leadership in such turbulent times, a new President of Boston University, Jon Westling, was named before the current President, John Silber, had stepped down. This was reported in Boston University's weekly newspaper, *Boston University Today* of January 23-29, 1995. It is also interesting to note that Boston University recognized the importance of continuity of leadership through the appointment of a "32 member blue ribbon Task Force on Continuity. . . . "

3. The terms "interim director" and "acting director" are not used in the profession consistently and are imbued with so much local meaning that I have not attempted to define or imply any differential in the use of the two terms. The reader should consider them synonymous.

4. Joanne R. Euster, and Eric Solomon, "In Praise of Acting and Permanent Library Directors and Their Symbiosis: A Dialog," *Library Trends,* 44 (Summer 1994): 136-43.

5. In order to elicit the most open comments from the individuals interviewed, they were assured that their comments would be reported without real or potential attribution.

6. It is interesting to note that many of those interviewed, either at the end of the interview or in later conversations with the author, used words such as therapeutic or cathartic to describe the interview.

7. Although there are a number of organizational models that apply, for ease of reading and writing and also because it is the most frequently valid case from my interviews, I have used the office and title of "provost" to refer to any senior administrator or board chairperson to whom the library director reports.

8. Here it should be noted that even in organizations where there exists the position of deputy director, that position usually exists to identify a chain of command for direct operational oversight and never as a command succession to the permanent directorship.

9. Euster and Solomon, "In Praise of Acting and Permanent Library Directors and Their Symbiosis: A Dialog."

10. Such non-traditional career endings are eloquently described in *The Age of Unreason* by Charles Handy (Boston Harvard Business School Press, 1990). See for example his discussion entitled, "The Third Age" which begins on p. 40.

APPENDIX

Questions to Interviewees

Please consider the following questions as guides for thinking about your interim period. I am, however, most interested in hearing your most vivid recollections about your interim period.

1. Tell me about becoming the interim director. How was the opportunity communicated to you? Were you given a clear charge? Were you well prepared/positioned for the role?

2. Tell me about being the interim director. Were you an activist director or a caretaker? What did you do to get started? What were the high and low points of being an operational leader?

3. Tell me about the period during the search. What was your role in the search? How did the search affect your leadership effectiveness and relations to the library staff?

4. Tell me about the aftermath of the search. How did the search affect you as an individual and as a professional?

5. What advice would you give to anyone considering accepting an offer to be the interim director of a research library?

Succession Paths
for Academic Library Directors

Karen A. Hatcher

INTRODUCTION

When Jack Welch, CEO of General Electric, experienced major health problems that affected his ability to continue in a leadership role the stock of GE did not take a nose dive. Why? People in the business world know that GE is a well-run company with a succession plan.

"Higher education does not tend to groom its future leaders, particularly within individual institutions, the way business organizations do."[1] You do not readily find programs in higher education entitled "The Succession Ladder to Dean or University President." Higher education, academic libraries included, provides mentoring and gives others a chance to obtain progressively higher level positions, but there is not a clear internal plan for obtaining a library director's position.

This article will study library literature to ascertain what the historical patterns have been for succession to the academic library director's position. A survey of middle-sized academic libraries as represented in the Council on State University Libraries will determine if there have been major changes in the succession patterns for

Karen A. Hatcher is Dean of Library Services, Mansfield Library, University of Montana, Missoula, MT (e-mail: hatcher@selway.umt.edu).

[Haworth co-indexing entry note]: "Succession Paths for Academic Library Directors." Hatcher, Karen A. Co-published simultaneously in the *Journal of Library Administration* (The Haworth Press, Inc.) Vol. 24, No. 3, 1997, pp. 31-46; and: *The Academic Library Director: Reflections on a Position in Transition* (ed: Frank D'Andraia) The Haworth Press, Inc., 1997, pp. 31-46. Single or multiple copies of this article are available for a fee from The Haworth Document Delivery Service [1-800-342-9678, 9:00 a.m. - 5:00 p.m. (EST). E-mail address: getinfo@haworth.com].

31

library directors. Finally, there will be a discussion on the reasons behind the statistical patterns observed for succession paths of library directors.

HISTORICAL BACKGROUND– LEARNING FROM THE PAST

A study of library literature ascertained there were different succession paths for men and women to reach the level of an academic library director. A study by W. C. Blankenship observed the best way for a male in the library profession to quickly obtain an administrative position was to be prepared to move to another library. In 1967 women did not change libraries as often as men; therefore, they did not become heads of libraries as quickly as men. Both of these studies were, of course, conducted during the formative years of the women's movement into upper management. Blankenship's study included 414 head librarians, almost equally divided between men and women. These librarians were in public and private colleges with enrollments of up to 5,000 students. One conclusion from his study was that male librarians were more likely to become head librarians in the larger publicly supported colleges. The study also showed women were more likely to be head librarians in smaller private colleges and promoted from within. However, " . . . women appear equally as capable, if not more capable than men, in getting funds for the library."[2]

In 1973, the image of women's ability to move into administrative positions was given a grim assessment by Wendy de Fichy: "Women's negative self-image is a major barrier to improvement in their status. The view of themselves as inferior and lacking in intellectual and other skills necessary for success prevents many women from trying and severely handicaps those who do."[3] De Fichy hoped the newly enacted affirmative action law would aid women in changing this image. It was five years after Blankenship's study that the federal equal opportunity law became applicable in institutions of higher education.

In his overview of ARL directors William L. Cohn found all four female ARL directors serving in 1973 were internal succession appointments. Cohn stated: "Despite evidence from several researchers that mobility is a key factor in promotion within the profession, it would appear that women can only reach the top rungs by staying put and 'proving' their abilities to those making the appointments. Further, it would appear that the increased size of the member libraries of ARL has led to a decreased number of female directors."[4]

Two further studies, done in the late 1970s, confirm Cohn's findings regarding the hiring patterns of large research libraries. Jerry Parsons compared the characteristics of research library directors in 1958 and 1973. "It didn't take much analysis to notice that women, in a field numerically dominated by women, were by 1973 attaining some of the leadership positions in large libraries."[5] Parsons made this statement because in the 1958 group of directors there were no women represented. By 1973 he had found the same four directors Cohn had noticed. Additionally, there was one woman filling an acting director's position. Parsons concluded that generally, the male directors in 1985 were more likely to be hired externally. This would appear to confirm Blankenship's 1967 observation. The finding obviously did not apply to women directors who were still finding internal promotion as the best way to the director's chair.

Paul Metz conducted an important study in 1978 that dealt strictly with administrative succession in the academic library. The study included data from 215 academic libraries of all sizes from four-year colleges through the Association of Research Libraries. Metz's goal was to find the most important aspects relating to succession by looking at the frequency of succession and the type of librarians chosen. Metz noted that the group he studied included more females than Parsons' study because Metz's survey did not confine itself to only the ARL group of institutions. While Metz had a larger proportion of female directors in his study, he came to the same conclusion as Cohn: " . . . women are three times as likely as men to have been hired to their directorships from within the library."[6] The tendency applied to women in both public and private institutions.

A study done five years later by Barbara B. Moran only confirmed the findings of Metz and Cohn: "One of the most surprising findings about the female directors was the high percentage who had become directors in the same library where they had previously served as assistant or associate directors."[7] Moran did find four female library directors hired as external candidates, but only one of these was in an academic library. The other three women became directors of nonacademic libraries.

Ronald Karr's research looked at the differences between ARL (Association for Research Libraries) directors in 1966 and 1981. He found 14 percent (12 positions) of the 1981 directorships filled by females. This represented a three-fold increase from the studies of Cohn and Parsons, but it was still far from equality when two-thirds of all academic librarians were female and only 14 percent were directors.

Several important studies were published in 1985. Foremost of these was the book by Betty Jo Irvine on *Sex Segregation in Librarianship*. Irvine supported the previous findings of internal succession for women. She noted internal succession not only applied to women library directors but also applied to women who became college presidents and corporate executives in the business world.

Moran followed up her earlier 1983 article with one in 1985 studying the influence of affirmative action on higher education and comparing the status of women in librarianship. This study was not confined to large research libraries but also drew on the next level of ACRL (Association of College & Research Libraries) and college libraries. She confirms Irvine's finding of a three-fold increase in women holding administration positions, at least in the ACRL size libraries. The 12 women directors in the large research libraries were still a minority compared to the number of women librarians. Private businesses could claim that they had fewer women in the lower rungs and therefore it would take longer for them to move into positions where they could gain the experience necessary for leadership positions. However, academic libraries have always had a large proportion of women in their positions. Why weren't they moving up at a faster rate? The 1982 ARL work force consisted of 62 percent females; however, 77 percent of library directors were male. Similar proportions were found for the Liberal Arts I institutions. Therefore, Moran concluded that while affirmative action has helped women move up into the mid-level administrative positions the law had not had much of an impact on the director level.

Altman and Promis added to the study in 1994 by examining the effect of affirmative action on academic librarianship. While they concentrated on whether affirmative action has really brought about a culturally diverse library staff, they studied the opportunities for acting directors to move into the position permanently. This study deals with several types of supervisory positions, not just the director's level. They found " . . . the candidates already acting in the job who applied had only slightly better than a fifty-fifty chance of appointment."[8] Of the 20 openings at the director's level, four, or 20 percent, were filled with acting candidates through an internal promotion.

Unfortunately Altman and Promis also found that women are still not applying for the higher administrative positions of director, associate director and department head as much as men. They were more likely to apply for the section head, branch librarian or deputy positions. They conclude, "Women were not chosen for higher-level positions in any greater numbers than their predecessors in these same positions. . . . It could be argued that the time of big gains for women has already occurred."[9]

Is this the case? The current study involves 21 ACRL level libraries. Some changes in the historical patterns were observed from the previous succession patterns used to reach library director's positions.

COSUL SURVEY

Purpose and Methodology

The purpose of this survey was to determine whether the succession path to become academic library director of ACRL-size libraries had changed from previous studies. In addition, the succession path for male and female librarians would be investigated. Has the influence of affirmative action or the mobility of today's family affected the previous succession paths? The research instrument was a simple one-page questionnaire faxed to the 21 library directors of The Council on State University Libraries. There were no vacancies or acting directors in these 21 positions. There was 100 percent return.

The Council on State University Libraries (COSUL)

COSUL involves 21 libraries that are the major research libraries in their states. Libraries involved are: University of Alaska (Fairbanks), University of Arkansas, Arkansas State University, University of Idaho, Idaho State University, University of Maine (Orono), University of Mississippi, Mississippi State University, University of Montana, Montana State University, University of Nevada-Reno, University of Nevada-Las Vegas, University of New Hampshire, University of North Dakota, University of Rhode Island, University of South Dakota, South Dakota State University, University of Vermont, West Virginia University, University of Wyoming. All these libraries are part of public ACRL institutions. There are no public ARL institutions in these states.

These 21 libraries have a wide range of missions, yet the largely rural nature of the states they serve gives them a commonality. Other unique factors to consider about the states concern size and population.

Table 1 clearly demonstrates the largest state with the lowest population density and the smallest state with the highest population density are part of COSUL. Half of the states fall into the top half of the country in the amount of rural areas; however, only two states fall into the top half for amount of urban areas. Six of the 14 states are east of the Mississippi River. All geographical areas of the country are represented in these states.

While the sample for this survey is small, it covers a distinct group of libraries that are the leading research libraries in their states. These 21 academic research libraries are located in 14 states, have significant rural populations and receive limited levels of federal research funding. Yet, these 21 academic research libraries must support research needs of a small and widely dispersed population without the resource base of larger research universities. These libraries are the lead institutions among the public institutions of higher education in their states; they have a state-wide role and mission. Many of the institutions have land grant status and are comprehensive universities with doctoral programs. Their lead institution status also makes them the major lender of information resources to all populations in their respective states.

TABLE 1. Population and Area of COSUL States

COSUL States	Population	People/Sq. Mile	Ranking in % of Rural Areas*	Ranking in % of Urban Areas**
Alaska	550,000	1.03	1	50
Arkansas	2,351,000	46.07	18	31
Idaho	1,007,000	12.89	6	45
Maine	1,228,000	40.01	19	32
Mississippi	2,573,000	55.72	21	30
Montana	799,000	5.66	2	47
Nevada	1,202,000	12.08	9	40
New Hampshire	1,109,000	123.87	38	12
North Dakota	639,000	9.22	3	47
Rhode Island	1,003,000	961.72	49	2
South Dakota	696,000	9.37	5	46
Vermont	563,000	61.63	14	37
West Virginia	1,793,000	75.23	15	36
Wyoming	454,000	4.8	4	47

* Rural Areas are defined as locations with populations less than 2,500 or open countryside.
** Urban areas are defined as locations with populations more than 2,500.

COSUL Library Statistics

What type of institutions and student body do these 21 libraries serve? In relation to the Carnegie Classification for Educational Institutions they range from Research I to Masters I. Enrollment ranges from 5,000 to over 22,000 students. The total library budgets range from $2,000,000 to over $6,000,000. Collection size ranges from 500,000 volumes to close to 2,000,000 volumes.

The main objective of the study was to determine if there had been any change in the previous patterns observed with internal succession. The 21 library directors were asked to provide the type of degree they had earned, their age when becoming director at the present library, number of years in their current position, whether they had been an in-house or external candidate and number of previous administrative positions.

RESULTS

Gender

Previous studies have shown it was easier for women to become a library director at smaller libraries. While these libraries are the largest in their states, they do represent the level below the ARL group. As Table 2 shows, of the 21 directorships, 6, or 28 percent are occupied by females. Metz's 1978 study included 215 institutions, mainly non-ARL universities. Women were directors in 10 of the 73 public academic libraries, representing 13 percent of the director's positions. Moran's comparative study looking at 92 non-ARL institutions in 1972 and 1982 showed a rise in the number of female library directors. In 1972 five females or 5.6 percent were directors. This increased to 16 females or 17.6 percent by 1982. Of the 54 public, non-ARL institutions studied by Wong and Zubatsky, 20 percent, or 11 institutions, had women directors in 1985. So there has been a slight gain of women in the positions of directors in the non-ARL group of institutions.

Degrees

The number and type of degrees have changed slightly from earlier studies according to Table 3. All 21 COSUL directors have earned a Master of Library Science degree, 8 directors have earned

TABLE 2. Responses According to the Sex of Library Directors

Library Directors	Number	Percent
Males	15	72.00%
Females	6	28.00%
Total	21	100.00%

TABLE 3. Degrees Earned

	Men/Number	Men/Percent	Women/Number	Women/Percent
M.L.S.	15	100%	6	100%
Subject M.S.	10	66%	0	0%
Ph.D.	3	20%	2	33%

a second Master's degree, 5 directors have earned doctorates, and 2 directors are working on doctorates. Four of the female directors only have the Master of Library Science, while the other 2 female directors, representing 9.5 percent of the total, have doctorates. This represents an increase over previous studies. Metz did not break down the degrees by sex and Moran did not add this factor into her study. Wong and Zubatsky did study degrees earned by type of library and sex. All 11 library directors had M.L.S. degrees, 5 percent had a second Master's degree, and 5 percent had doctorates.

Age

Table 4 provides the age when the COSUL directors obtained their present position. The ages range from 33 to 58 with 45 the average age. The average age of female directors is 45, the mean 47. For the 15 male directors the average age is 52, the mean 54. Metz found the average age of his directors to be 47.5 years. Earlier studies found the opposite results. Generally men became directors at an earlier age and women at a later age. Blankenship's study found the average age of male directors to fall into the 31-40 years category. For females the average age was in the 50 and over category.

Tenure

The length the COSUL directors have been in their current position varied from 3 months to 24 years. The average was almost 7 years with the mean being 5 years according to Table 5. The female library directors have been directors for an average and mean of 5 years. The men have an average of 8 years as directors with a mean

TABLE 4. Age When Present Position Obtained

Age Range	Male	Female
30-35	1	
36-40		2
41-45	8	
46-50	4	4
51-55	1	
56-60	1	

TABLE 5. Number of Years as Director in Current Library

	Males	Females
Less than 1 year	2	1
1-2 years	1	1
3-4 years	5	
5-6 years	2	3
7-8 years		
9-10 years	1	
11-12 years	2	
13-14 years	1	1
15-20 years		
21 or more years	1	

of 4.5. This data is comparable to that of Wong and Zubatsky; however, it disagrees with Parsons' 1973 study. He found the average length in a current position to be 12 years for ARL directors in both 1958 and 1973. The shorter length of tenure has been the subject of several studies including the McAnally and Downs article in 1973 discussing the changing tenure of library directors.

The current study demonstrates tenure has not lengthened much in the ACRL group.

Succession Paths

The number of internal succession hires among the 21 COSUL directors reflects a new trend compared to earlier studies. As Table 6 demonstrates of the 21 director positions, 6, or 29 percent, were filled with librarians who had previously held administrative positions within the same library. An interesting finding in this study is that of these 6 internal hires, only 2 were female librarians with 4 being filled with male librarians through internal succession. Thus, of the 21 director positions, 9.5 percent were internal promotions of females and 19 percent were internal promotions of males. This is a major difference from other studies. Of the external hires, 4 positions were obtained by women librarians, or 27 percent of the external hires went to women. Two-thirds of the pool of 6 female library directors obtained their positions through external hire.

This represents a definite increase over previous studies but still falls short when considering the total proportion of women librarians in the profession. Metz found in looking at both public and private libraries that 54 percent of the women were internal hires and only 17 percent of the men were internal hires. When focusing only on public institutions, about 50 percent of the women librarians were internal hires and 11 percent of the men were internal hires. Wong and Zubatsky found 6 percent of the women and 16 percent of the men were promoted from within their library to the director's position. There has been a definite shift in the percentages with more men being hired through internal succession and women obtaining a higher percentage of external succession positions.

TABLE 6. Internal/External Succession

	Males - #	Males - %	Females - #	Females - %
External	11	73.33%	4	66.66%
Internal	4	26.67%	2	33.34%

Professional Experience

Previous academic experience varied. Most of the librarians in this study had from one to three previous administrative positions. One or two had even been directors at other libraries before their present position. The female directors averaged two other administrative positions before obtaining their current director's position, and the male directors averaged 3 previous administrative positions. Only a few had been librarians in other types of libraries: school, public and military. About one-fourth of the previous positions had been in the technical services area of academic libraries. The rest were public service oriented with a few being branch librarians. Almost always the current director's position was a move up either from a mid-level administrative position or from director of a smaller library. Only the male directors had been directors at other academic libraries.

COSUL Survey Findings

Statistically this study shows there has been a change in the administrative accession path for non-ARL public libraries. Women are finding it easier to apply for and obtain library director positions through external hires. Male librarians no longer have to move to obtain a library director position.

SUBJECTIVE REASONS BEHIND THE STATISTICS

The historical survey of library literature on the topic of academic library director succession and the current survey of COSUL librarians give statistical reasons for the different succession paths provided for women and men to reach an academic library director position. The COSUL study provides evidence of changing patterns in these succession paths. Women librarians are applying for and obtaining directorships as external candidates. Male librarians no longer have the path of internal promotion closed to them. What has changed in the last 30 years to alter the succession path to obtaining an academic library directorship?

De Fichy's earlier survey laid the problem of women's advancement on her negative self-image. Women librarians viewed themselves as inferior and lacking in the necessary skills for success and this prevented them from applying for directorships. De Fichy also observed the low salaries paid to women librarians made them more dependent on the husband's higher paying jobs. Blankenship noticed that women did not change jobs as often as men and he had already stated that a librarian had to change positions in order to advance. He hinted that marriage might have an impact on this. In her 1983 study, Moran warned if the hiring patterns did not change the ambitious woman wanting to become an academic library director would have to passively wait for her present institution to notice her. She would find the avenue of being hired by another institution closed to her.

Early studies showed that women were able to obtain positions as directors in small, private colleges, whereas the males were directors in the larger ARL groups. It was suggested this was because a woman took longer to prove herself as a manager and had to do this within the library she would be hired to manage. The previous studies hypothesized that academic libraries were not willing to take a chance on an unknown person with unproved management ability. Academic libraries that wanted a library director who would maintain the "status quo" and not come in and change everything might feel a female librarian who had proven management qualities in assistant director or department head positions would be a safe person to hire. Male librarians were viewed as administrators who would come in and change the "status quo." Also, an internal candidate could be paid a lower salary.

Today's family, with both the husband and wife working, is still mobile. There are many instances in which a family moves for a promotion of either the wife's or husband's job. So changes in society can be looked at to explain part of the changes in the ability of women to obtain externally hired director positions and men to obtain internal succession director positions.

If you look at the six internal hires versus the 15 external hires in the COSUL group, geography could be examined to explain the difference in the internal versus external hires. All six internal hires, whether male or female, are in libraries west of the Mississippi

River and in states of a rural nature. As an earlier researcher hinted, internal hires can be acquired at a lower pay. Positions in rural states generally are less competitive than those in urban areas. Pay could be lower because of a lower cost of living or because of lower competition for the positions. Neither of these factors were investigated in the COSUL study, although all geographic areas of the country were covered by COSUL libraries. So while the earlier barriers to succession paths might be crumbling new barriers are being built. This would be an interesting issue for future studies. Is the supposition that an external male director would find it easier to affect change within a new library than an internal female hire really valid? Do organizations fear the management ability of an external female candidate more than a male? These are very subjective ideas and hard to validate but the answers would benefit all candidates for positions of an academic library directorship.

When asked for opinions on an internal succession path versus an external path COSUL library directors had mixed views. Several directors felt strongly the overriding concern was the general qualification of the person being hired for the vacant position rather than whether the person was an internal or external candidate. An internal candidate obviously is familiar with the institution, the library, faculty and staff and the institution is familiar with the candidate. There are fewer risks in hiring a known candidate. This can give the internal candidate an advantage to adapt faster than an external candidate. The negative sides of being an internal candidate are the problems that might exist or had existed in the past are still with the candidate even as they move up the career ladder. The external candidate can serve as an agent for change and bring experience from other institutions.

OUTSIDE THE LIBRARY

Has succession planning made a difference for women in the private sector? A cursory study of any information database will provide hundreds of articles on the current existence of a "glass ceiling." There is even a U.S. Federal Glass Ceiling Commission.

Are women librarians behind women in other positions in reaching the "CEO" position of academic libraries? A few comparisons will illustrate that women do not fare any better in other areas. Women have moved into the general work force in greater numbers since the 1970s. Overall, women hold 46 percent of the jobs available in the work force; yet, only 5 percent are top executives. Women account for 52.8 percent of all professional occupations including engineers, lawyers, architects, dentists and physicians. They hold 48.1 percent of the managerial or executive positions in these professions, but they occupy only 3 percent of the senior management positions.

In most occupations women have had to take the time to occupy increasingly responsible positions at lower administrative and managerial rungs on the ladder. This might account for the low number of women in executive positions. Elementary and secondary education have long been occupied by women, as has librarianship; however, the administrative positions are predominantly occupied by males. In K-12 education, 89 percent of the school superintendents and high school principals are men. So the number of women superintendents and principals is not much greater than women library directors.

Darla J. Twale, in a speech to the Eastern Educational Research Association in 1992, analyzed the administrative appointments of women in higher education. From 1986 to 1991, despite the use of affirmative action in the public education area, Twale found more women hired in higher positions by private educational institutions than public institutions. She concluded private education institutions had more flexible hierarchies and were more willing to hire a female based on her competence and expertise, not just the credentials of the previous position.

Private industry has succession planning, and other professions might be influenced by affirmative action regulation, but the "glass ceiling" still exists. The predominance of women in a profession such as school teaching or librarianship seems to have had little influence on the number of women serving in top administrative positions.

FUTURE RESEARCH

The sample used for this study was small. Would the findings be the same for a larger sample? Is there a difference between the type of library directors hired by ARL, ACRL and the Oberlin group? Does geography or competitive salary make a difference in choosing an internal candidate versus an external candidate? Are male library directors really better at changing the direction of academic libraries? Hopefully forthcoming studies will reveal continuing change in succession paths for academic library directors.

NOTES

1. Person, Ruth J. and George Charles Newman, "Selection of the University Librarian," *College & Research Libraries* 51 (1990): 346-359.

2. Blankenship, W.C., "Head librarians: how many men? How many women?" *College & Research Libraries* 28 (1967): 41-48.

3. Fichy, Wendy, "Affirmative action: equal opportunity for women in library management," *College & Research Libraries* 34 (1973): 195-201.

4. Cohn, William L., "An Overview of ARL directors, 1933-1973," *College & Research Libraries* 37 (1976): 137-144.

5. Parsons, Jerry, "How have they changed? Characteristics of research library directors, 1958 and 1973," *Wilson Library Bulletin* 50 (1976): 613-617.

6. Metz, Paul, "Administrative succession in the academic library," *College & Research Libraries* 39 (1978): 358-364.

7. Moran, Barbara, "Career patterns of academic library administrators," *College & Research Libraries* 44 (1983): 334-344.

8. Altman, Ellen and Patricia Promis, "Affirmative action: opportunity or obstacle," *College & Research Libraries* 55 (1994): 11-23.

9. Ibid.

Recruiting a Library Leader
for the 21st Century

Rebecca R. Martin

Given the changing paradigm of higher education and the rapid development of the information society, the recruitment of a new library director is an opportunity to reshape the role of the library in the evolving university. New demands in information technology, increased investments in distance education, and emerging models of support for research and teaching have combined with a declining base of resources for universities to place academic libraries at a critical juncture. These interrelated forces require a fundamental rethinking and redesign of library roles, services, and operations in universities which are also undergoing great change. The library dean or director is in a key position to lead this transformation. This paper explores the evolving shape of academic libraries, the impact of this change on the role of the library director, and the orientation and qualifications.

HIGHER EDUCATION: A CHANGING LANDSCAPE

Rapid, far-reaching change is emerging as the dominant pattern in our society as we enter the twenty-first century. Whether we

Rebecca R. Martin is Dean of Libraries, University of Vermont, Burlington, VT (e-mail: rebecca.martin@uvm.edu).

[Haworth co-indexing entry note]: "Recruiting a Library Leader for the 21st Century." Martin, Rebecca R. Co-published simultaneously in the *Journal of Library Administration* (The Haworth Press, Inc.) Vol. 24, No. 3, 1997, pp. 47-58; and: *The Academic Library Director: Reflections on a Position in Transition* (ed: Frank D'Andraia) The Haworth Press, Inc., 1997, pp. 47-58. Single or multiple copies of this article are available for a fee from The Haworth Document Delivery Service [1-800-342-9678, 9:00 a.m. - 5:00 p.m. (EST). E-mail address: getinfo@haworth.com].

47

consider models for industry, for government, or for information, the common theme today is change. Rosabeth Moss Kanter asserts that in the coming decade, responding to change, harnessing change, and creating change will become the major challenges for organizations.[1] The organizations that survive will be those that view change as an opportunity rather than as a threat.

> Higher education is under significant pressure to make major changes in the nature of its institutional structures and academic offerings. As Peter Smith has noted, external forces are dramatically changing the public's aspirations and expectations vis-à-vis higher education institutions. And the system's perceived inability to respond effectively is seriously eroding public confidence.[2]

Alan Guskin points to the "double-edged sword of costs" as driving many of these forces. The expenses of colleges and universities have exceeded their revenues, and the resulting costs are beyond students' and their families' capability and willingness to pay. He identifies three major forces which will alter our universities in the next decade:

1. High costs associated with undergraduate education in the public and private sectors will give way to overwhelming pressures to cut back tuition rather than increase expenses.
2. There will be an ever-growing demand from many sectors of society that we document and improve student learning outcomes.
3. The new information technology will provide the capability to alter how students learn and how faculty teach.[3]

The realization and acknowledgment of this emerging strategic context has prompted many higher education and political leaders to conclude that the postsecondary institutions that enter the next century will be dramatically changed from those we know today.[4] The juxtaposition of the pressure to reduce costs with the need to invest in new student-centered and technology-based approaches to education requires a fundamental reordering of institutional priorities and redesign of organizational structures.

For the academic library, the ramifications of this strategic context for higher education are familiar but profound. As a focal point for information in the institution, the library has been an early innovator in information technology. Likewise, the increasing emphasis on student consumerism does not present an unfamiliar challenge for libraries, as the focus on users and their needs has dominated the development of library services for the past several decades. However, the pressures of these advances in the face of spiraling costs of information sources and reductions in institutional support have forced the significant questioning of longstanding principles and practices throughout library services and operations.

In this complex environment, managing change becomes a critical component of leadership. Peter Drucker states that "for managers, the dynamics of knowledge impose one clear imperative: every organization has to build the management of change into its very structure."[5] The stable, rule-oriented structures of traditional organizations must give way to more fluid forms capable of responding to new demands. As Susan Lee points out, management's focus should be on designing and bringing into being the institutional processes through which new problems can continually be confronted and old structures continually discarded.[6] Furthermore, the anticipation of change is crucial. In health care, currently an extremely volatile and chaotic environment, those leaders who are responding to market forces rather than hedging their bets are moving too slowly to be effective;[7] there may be lessons here for higher education as well.

For university libraries to thrive in this new environment, they must capitalize upon change in order to maintain their central roles in the institutions they serve. Many have written about the opportunities for new roles for libraries in academe and these will not be covered here.[8] However, the implications for library organizations and those that direct them are paramount and deserving of further exploration.

THE LIBRARY DIRECTOR: MANAGER OR LEADER?

The academic library director has traditionally been viewed as a manager, albeit of a large and important operation within the university. This director manages budgets, directs people, builds libraries, and plans for incremental growth in programs and resources. To interface with various campus constituencies is important, but it is often limited to issues which relate directly to the library.

Today's environment demands more of library directors than this traditional managerial role, which is archaic and can seriously retard change. As the environment becomes more complex, library directors must become equally complex if they are to sense changes and design appropriate adaptations.[9] Irene Hoadley sees the potential for library directors to develop as leaders rather than managers, exhibiting creativity, risk taking, innovation, and intuition in approaching both the goals and the operations of the library.[10] A major role for the library director in campus restructuring is also emerging, as issues of information technology, distance education, and student-centered focus move to the forefront of institutional agendas. The shift on many campuses to the academic leadership title of dean in lieu of library director may be a harbinger of this change.

The distinction between managers and leaders has been the topic of many management theorists. A noted expert in this field, Warren Bennis, differentiates between managers and leaders in these ways:

- The manager administers, the leader innovates.
- The manager focuses on systems and structure; the leader focuses on people.
- The manager asks how and when; the leader asks what and why.
- The manager does things right; the leader does the right thing.[11]

While there is clearly still a need for managers in academic libraries, a more complex and expansive role for the library director may be required for the challenges ahead.

A review of recent job announcements for college and university library directors and deans revealed some movement towards the conception of this role as a leader, but most continued to characterize the duties and qualifications of the position in terms more descriptive of managers. Of the twenty-three such advertisements appearing in *College and Research Libraries News* in 1995, only a third called for roles or qualifications which might be associated with leaders in this changing environment. Notable statements from these job announcements include:

- a vision of the role innovative information technologies can play in higher education as well as an understanding of the changing paradigm in scholarly communication; will be expected to create an organizational structure and a working environment that encourage creativity, cost effectiveness, and change;
- a skilled, imaginative and flexible approach to the use of new information technologies; a vision of how these technologies can be combined with more traditional library resources;
- demonstrated leadership/management in integrating and advancing innovative programs in response to a changing technological and informational environment;
- a clear understanding of the evolving role of the academic research library and changes in scholarly communication, the important role of cooperation and resource sharing, and library automation and new information technologies;
- evidence of managerial vision, strong creative leadership, problem-solving aptitude, broad and effective communication;
- commitment to a flexible, proactive, organizational environment;
- successful experience with organizational change;
- ability to guide the development of the rapidly developing innovations in information technology;
- an energetic and visionary leader.

These requirements suggest a recognition of the contributions libraries will make in a restructured university and the enlarged role for library directors as leaders of organizations in transition. Before considering the characteristics of such leaders in more detail, new organizational models in academic libraries will be examined.

MODELS FOR EMERGING LIBRARY ORGANIZATIONS

The significant changes occurring in academic libraries have been characterized by some as nothing short of organizational transformation. Shelley Phipps captures the essence of this transformation in a concrete way, stating that libraries

> are being transformed from collection centered organizations to access organizations; from repositories of the printed format to organizations that are less tied to place, to paper, and to print. They are linking users to information held locally or available remotely, and empowering users to become self-sufficient information finders . . . the roles played by the library in the scholarly communication process are becoming more proactive, assertive, and collaborative.[12]

Organizational change in support of this transformation is taking many forms, and most often managers in complex organizations are likely to face the prospect of working within multiple organizational models.[13]

Richard Sweeney describes an ideal type for the radical redesign of academic libraries which he has dubbed the post-hierarchical library.[14] Although he admits that no library has fully achieved reengineering to this degree, he sees this entirely new organization of redesigned work processes as the form of the future. The very nature of library services, library work, and library leadership would be fundamentally changed in this model. This anti-bureaucratic library would be focused on user services, less bound by inflexible rules and the tradition of paperwork, and able to adapt to meet changing needs.

The post-hierarchical library would be characterized by a flattened organizational structure, empowered cross-functional teams, fewer people, constant learning, reduced operations, and new reliance on local and national information infrastructures. The central feature of networked teams would require more communication, more distributed decision making, and better methods for accountability.

The role of the library leader would become that of a strategist with a vision, a plan, and the will to achieve it. Sweeney sees the need for continuing with the traditional library as it declines in importance, but promotes the strategic and rapid shifting of resources into the reinvented, post-hierarchical library.

Voicing many of these themes and drawing heavily upon the

work of Peter Senge, Shelley Phipps espouses the model of the learning organization for the emerging academic library.[15] She finds the transformational process of the learning organization, which is guided by an understanding of the basic purpose of an organization and where it is going, to be particularly relevant to libraries. The reliance on people's commitment and capacity to learn at all levels of the organization works well with the team-based management structures found in many evolving library organizations.

In his seminal work, *The Fifth Discipline,* Senge defines a learning organization as a place where people are continually discovering how they create their reality and how they can change it. He identifies five disciplines which together form the necessary ensemble for all members of the organization:

1. Personal mastery: clarifying personal vision, connection to organizational values, individual self-fulfillment
2. Building shared visions: expanding collaborative capabilities to shape the future, fostering the collective ability to learn
3. Mental models: bringing to the surface and challenging prevailing mental models, creating new paradigms
4. Team learning: building upon the ideas of others, thinking together and insightfully about complex issues
5. Systems thinking: fostering systemic patterns of thinking, a holistic view of the organization, integration of the five disciplines.[16]

This new organization is a community of people continuously expanding their individual and collective capacity to create desired results.

Phipps finds that the limitations of today's organizations identified by Senge as barriers to this transformation are all present in academic libraries: linear thinking, controlling leadership, negative mental models, lack of vision, and individual competition. However, with appropriate leadership and organizational commitment to change, she asserts that the model of the learning organization has great potential for libraries.[17]

Susan Lee has also written very thoughtfully about organizational change in research libraries, posing a model of her own for consideration.[18] In dealing with our need to change, she asserts that we must go beyond defining our role in society to redefining our organization for carrying out that role. Her approach, grounded in the literature of organizational development, stresses seven factors: raising the level of generality, creating integrative vehicles to enhance flexibility, emphasizing organizational culture and values, considering a political perspective, replacing strategic planning with strategic organizational change, training for behavioral competence, and building organizational units or teams.

Organizational flexibility, dealing with uncertainty, and living with organizational change play a role in each of these strategies. Of utmost importance is her approach to organizational change, which she distills in this statement:

> To effectively manage in today's changing environment, an understanding of how change is designed and constructed in an organization, how small changes relate to strategic reorientations, is required.[19]

Change is seen as an ongoing, essential element in the functioning of the organization.

While none of these models can be explicitly identified in today's academic libraries, their elements may be found in many libraries as organizational modifications are made in response to a changing environment. In some cases, specific approaches such as Total Quality Management (TQM) or team-based management have been fully embraced; in others, organizational streamlining or outsourcing of certain functions have led to redirection and reconfiguration of services and resources. If there is one common theme, it is that change has become a constant for academic libraries and is likely to remain so for the foreseeable future.

NEW ROLES FOR NEW LEADERS

The library director of the twenty-first century is likely to lead an organization which will evolve to one very different from the academic library of today. The ability to manage change, both within the library and in the broader campus environment, has become a crucial skill for these leaders. The theories and models explored above suggest some new functions and qualifications for library leaders. In addition, the earlier assertion that in recruiting library directors we should now be seeking leaders rather than managers results in a different set of desirable characteristics or skills than may have been previously sought.

Turning again to the leadership expert Warren Bennis, we find a concise set of competencies for leaders. Above all, Bennis finds that the best leaders "know themselves; they know their strengths and nurture them." His leadership competencies, which are universal enough to apply to any leadership role, include:

1. Management of Attention: the leader moves through a set of intentions or vision to a sense of outcome, goals, and direction.
2. Management of Meaning: the leader makes dreams apparent to others and aligns people with communication and teamwork.
3. Management of Trust: the leader is characterized by a sense of reliability and constancy.
4. Management of Self: the leader knows his/her skills and deploys them effectively, and is ever self-critical.[20]

Set in the context of a changing organization, perhaps utilizing one of the models described above, these competencies carry the common themes of vision, communication, and trust.

In Peter Senge's learning organization, the leader is a designer, a teacher, and a steward of the shared vision. Roles for leaders who may be at various levels in the organization include introducing a new organizational culture, empowering individuals, developing teams and work groups, setting new standards for quality, redefining the organizational structure, building networks, and developing strategic vision.[21]

James Penrod and Michael Dolence tailor Senge's model to a reengineered university and emphasize the leader's ability to: vividly articulate a shared vision, balance inquiry and advocacy, discern between espoused theory and actual practice, defuse defensive routines and resistance to change, see interrelationships and not focus on detail, avoid symptomatic solutions, and act as an agent of change. Above all, the leader in the information arena should be a knowledge seeker and a transfer agent, providing solutions to problems without waiting for new technology or enhanced resources.[22]

In the rapidly changing environment of academic libraries, another pivotal skill is the capacity to deal with uncertainty without losing sight of the vision. Susan Lee builds on this idea of cognitive complexity, stating that

> Effective leaders know the direction in which they are headed. Their organization's strategic vision provides the compass but not the road map. . . . The cognitively complex executive is the flexible thinker, making decisions on the run, decisions that are based on, and revised because of, new information.[23]

The dynamic nature of external forces and internal demands facing academic libraries lend credence to this picture of the library leader as one among a team of talented and engaged individuals, perhaps serving as the spark or focal point for forward movement and change.

Richard Sweeney's post-hierarchical library calls for a leader who is a superb communicator with good analytical skills, deductive and reasoning ability, and a sense of humor. These people will be pioneers who are willing to take carefully calculated risks with both their careers and the library to transform it into an organization that is a quantum leap beyond the previous organization.[24]

Library directors in the twenty-first century will be faced with unprecedented change in all aspects of their endeavors. Whether leading a learning organization or functioning in a reengineered university, these individuals will be called upon to make fundamental decisions about the future of their libraries. As transformational leaders, they can be expected to move libraries from their current situations to a new future, create visions of potential opportunities, instill new cultures and strategies, and mobilize the energy and resources of the staff.[25] Effective library leaders will also have the opportunity to take a leadership role in organizational change at the campus level, becoming important assets to the institution as a whole while libraries and universities undergo the paradigm shifts forecast for higher education in the next decade.

In this changing environment, the perspective on required credentials for these leaders may begin to change. Clearly, the skills described above were not part of the traditional library science masters programs completed by many librarians currently working in academic libraries. Some of the more innovative library leaders in colleges and universities today have advanced degrees in fields other than library science. While a firm understanding of library and information science is still imperative, the ability to bring new approaches to these issues, to "think outside the box," may become more important than a specific set of academic credentials.

It is essential that in selecting new leaders, we seek the innovative, creative risk takers described by Sweeney with the flexibility and cognitive complexity of Lee's effective executive. "People skills" will continue to be critical, as will the ability to articulate and convey a compelling vision for the library. Technical expertise will remain pertinent, at least in the form of a broad understanding of the issues and the potential for development. More relevant than a specific set of experiences will be the ability to learn, as the landscape continues to shift and new demands emerge.

If libraries are to maintain their central place in the academic endeavors of the university, we must create vital and viable roles for our faculty, staff, and services which build upon the new technology of information. We must redesign our organizations to respond to change and function within restructured institutions, most likely with a declining base of resources. Working together with library leaders, we can build upon our expertise and craft new libraries for our changing institutions.

NOTES

1. Rosabeth Moss Kanter, *The Challenge of Organizational Change* (New York: The Free Press, 1992).

2. *Educational Record* 72 (Spring 1991): 26-28.

3. Alan Guskin. "Reducing Student Costs and Enhancing Student Learning," *Change* 26 (1994): 22-29.

4. James I. Penrod and Michael G. Dolence, *Reengineering: A Process for Transforming Higher Education* (Boulder Colorado: CAUSE, 1992), 12.

5. Peter Drucker, *Managing in a Time of Great Change* (New York: Truman Talley Books/Dutton, 1995), 79.

6. Susan Lee, "Organizational Change in Research Libraries," *Journal of Library Administration* 18 (1993): 129-143.

7. Jill L. Sherer, "Managing Chaos," *Hospitals and Health Networks* 69 (Feb 20, 1995): 22-23+.

8. See, for example, Richard Lucier, "Knowledge Management: Refining Roles in Scientific Communication," in *New Technologies and New Directions* (Westport, CT: Meckler Publishing, 1993) and Sheila Creth, "A Changing Profession: Central Roles for Academic Librarians," *Advances in Librarianship* 19 (1995): 85-98.

9. Susan Lee, "Leadership: Revised and Redesigned for the Electronic Age," *Journal of Library Administration* 20 (1994): 17-28.

10. Irene B. Hoadley, "The Library Director; Introduction," *Library Trends* 43 (Summer 1994): 3-14.

11. Warren Bennis, "Managing the Dream: Leadership in the 21st Century," *Training* 27 (May 1990): 44-49.

12. Shelley E. Phipps, "Transforming Libraries into Learning Organizations–The Challenge for Leadership," *Journal of Library Administration* 18 (1993): 19-37.

13. Joan Giesecke, "Recognizing and Managing Multiple Organizational Approaches," *Journal of Library Administration* 20 (1994): 29-46.

14. Richard T. Sweeney, "Leadership in the Post-Hierarchical Library," *Library Trends* 43 (Summer 1994): 62-94.

15. Phipps, 19-37.

16. Peter Senge, *The Fifth Discipline: The Art and Practice of the Learning Organization* (New York: Doubleday, 1990).

17. Phipps, 24-25.

18. Lee, "Organizational Change in Research Libraries."

19. Ibid., 140.

20. Warren Bennis, *Why Leaders Can't Lead* (San Francisco: Jossey-Bass, 1989), 14-24.

21. Peter Senge, "The Leader's New Work: Building Learning Organizations," *Sloan Management Review* 32 (Fall 1990): 7-19+.

22. Penrod and Dolence, 18, 23.

23. Lee, "Leadership," 22.

24. Sweeney, 85-86.

25. Donald E. Riggs and Vivian M. Sykes, "The Time for Transformational Leadership is Now!" *Journal of Library Administration* 18 (1993): 55-68.

The Library, Information, and Institutional Outcomes: Searching in a Time of Change

Barbara Brittingham

Searching for a key university administrator is inherently challenging. Hiring the wrong person can easily cost an institution a quarter of a million dollars before the mistake is rectified; hiring a marginally successful person can cost much more. The time of the search committee, the direct costs of the search, the opportunity costs of hiring a less-than-ideal candidate, and the personal and professional costs to the unsuccessful candidate all come in addition. In several fields, certainly including libraries and information technologies, the work, context, and possibilities are changing so quickly that candidates with sufficient administrative seasoning for senior positions must have developed interests, knowledge, and skills that go far beyond what the leaders in their fields had 20 years ago. When a position is newly created, or significantly changed from the post held by the prior incumbent, the challenge is increased. Yet hiring the "right person"–or more realistically *a* right person–can easily be worth the work and the risk. Particularly so when, as with libraries, the field is changing rapidly, and the right hire can help the institution meet the coming challenges.

Barbara Brittingham is Dean, College of Human Sciences and Services, University of Rhode Island, Kingston, RI (e-mail: bbritt@uriacc.uri.edu).

[Haworth co-indexing entry note]: "The Library, Information, and Institutional Outcomes: Searching in a Time of Change." Brittingham, Barbara. Co-published simultaneously in the *Journal of Library Administration* (The Haworth Press, Inc.) Vol. 24, No. 3, 1997, pp. 59-71; and: *The Academic Library Director: Reflections on a Position in Transition* (ed: Frank D'Andraia) The Haworth Press, Inc., 1997, pp. 59-71. Single or multiple copies of this article are available for a fee from The Haworth Document Delivery Service [1-800-342-9678, 9:00 a.m. - 5:00 p.m. (EST). E-mail address: getinfo@haworth.com].

This article describes how the University of Rhode Island conducted its search for a newly configured position of Vice Provost for Information and Dean of University Libraries. Special emphasis is given to the interest of the institution in establishing a new academic administrative position that could serve the needs of the administration and of the faculty.

LOCAL CONTEXT

With 12,000 students on three campuses (a main campus in Kingston, the Narragansett Bay campus housing the Graduate School of Oceanography, and a continuing education campus in Providence), the University of Rhode Island is a land-, sea- and urban-grant institution and Rhode Island's publicly supported research university.

In 1992, the Provost appointed an Interim Dean of the University Libraries, charged to explore how the University might coordinate its library, computing, and instructional technology functions to improve support for the university mission of instruction, research, and academic outreach. The Interim Dean was appointed from outside the Library—the Dean of one of the University's professional colleges, and someone without prior work experience in a library. In making this appointment, the Provost indicated her belief that because of the substantial changes underway in libraries and technology, an independent look at the challenges and opportunities from someone with a broad range of experiences at the institution would be useful.

The Interim Dean appointed a 24-member committee to help educate the campus community on the issues and options. Midway through the work, due to other questions being raised within the institution, the committee took on the additional charge of recommending whether the University should establish the position, by whatever title, of chief information officer.

The committee, Chaired by the Interim Dean, included: librarians; staff from the computer centers (academic and administrative), audiovisual services, and instructional development; faculty members from oceanography, computer science and philosophy, plant science, art, speech, English, and economics; and library directors from two members of URI's principal library consortium. Knowledge of and experience with libraries and technology varied among committee members. The perspective of the user was prominent in the committee. With 10 of 24 members from the faculty, the committee was focused on ensuring that University resources and priorities in the general area of libraries, computers, and media were directed toward the teaching, research, and outreach needs of faculty and students. In terms of technology expertise, the committee ranged from professors who did not have e-mail addresses to a well-funded researcher who talked about the work that "my systems people" could do.

The committee functioned partly as a seminar, with members from the library, computing, and media staff serving to educate the body in the emerging technologies of the field as well as the historic roots of the area. While decisions of the history and current dilemmas of each function highlighted the unique contributions of each area, the committee could not escape the conclusion that anyone starting a new campus today would certainly ensure an integrated operation of libraries, computers, and media.

With the vision of seamless integration of information resources as a way to meet the academic mission of institutions, the committee recommended enhanced coordination between and among the related functions of libraries, computers, and instructional technology. The committee also recommended a fairly standard updating of the Dean of Libraries position, recognizing that the search committee, when one was appointed, would draft or work with an updated job description to be approved by the Provost and President. Due principally to the University budget situation, the Committee did not recommend adding new administrative positions (including a chief information officer) "at this time." The committee recommendations were conservative, a not-uncommon path for large university committees, with perhaps an extra dose of reluctance from some staff in each of the areas who were concerned that they may have more to lose than to gain under a more significant reconfiguration.

Meanwhile, on many fronts, the University administration was seeking to advance greater coordination of administrative units and to combine smaller units into larger entities to promote efficiency and coordination. With the advice of the above committee, consisting of chief academic officers from other universities, other off-campus advisors, and the Interim Dean, the Provost moved to reconfigure the position of Dean of University Libraries to become a Vice Provost for Information and Dean of University Libraries. With the title of Dean, the newly hired person would serve as the chief academic and administrative officer of the Library. With the title of Vice Provost for Information, the person would become a member of the Provost's staff, with institution-wide responsibilities for the coordination and support of the academic information resources, including libraries, academic computing, and instructional technology. In announcing her decision, the Provost also indicated that the newly hired administrator would have the opportunity to appoint someone to oversee the day-to-day operations of the Library.

While such position redefinitions may be increasingly common, the Provost's decision was, in some respects, at the beginning of what might be termed the "second wave" of such combinations on college campuses. What were the salient factors for such reorganizations? Three emerge: need, opportunity, and risk.

Clearly, there was a *need* for the University to address the challenges of gaining the greatest power and impact from key administrative appointments, regardless of the field. Public higher education in New England, while strong in many ways, is simply not funded at the levels of the large midwest public universities nor at the levels of the wealthiest independent institutions in the region. In the earlier times, and to greater and lesser extents depending on resources and style, institutions solved pressing organizational problems by adding faculty lines or creating new administrative and staff positions. Those days are over. Today—and clearly recognizing that institutional circumstance differs—colleges and universities must solve their problems with greater elegance and greater restraint: appointing one person to solve multiple related problems is a key strategy.

The University also faced an *opportunity*. A key position on our campus—many would argue *the* key position—in the constellation of libraries, computers, and media was vacant. Our chief librarian has traditionally served as a dean. We have also had a limited number of dean positions that serve concurrently as vice provosts: appointments that have the line responsibility of dean and the staff responsibility of vice provost. When the staff responsibility was added to the line position, the newly reconfigured position offered the provost more: more administrative help, and more staff support in an area key to the institution's future.

Finally, there was *risk*. Previously the University had used a traditional structure and had employed Library deans who had served the Library and the institution well. Changing a pattern that has provided sufficient success is inherently risky. The University's closest peer group, the New England land-grant institutions, had not elected the new path, at least yet (and one of them has subsequently elected to pursue a more traditional path), though it is clear that they discussed this topic. Searches for key administrators these days are fraught with challenge. Success requires clarity on the part of the institution for what it wants, a perceived opportunity among desired candidates, a willingness to actively recruit for the position, and some measure of good fortune (including the timing that attracts good candidates). A wealth of resources—not available in this case—may help. Clearly, there was risk involved in the Provost's decision; knowing the risk, she elected to take it.

THE SEARCH COMMITTEE AND THE POSITION

The Provost appointed a 16-member search committee charged to recommend a job description, and with this approval, search for and recommend no fewer than three candidates for the position. The Provost joined the first meeting of the search committee to discuss the position and opportunities for the new hire and for the institution.

The search committee was broadly constituted to do its job. Chaired by the Interim Dean of the University Libraries (who was not a librarian), the committee included representatives of the University Libraries (librarians and staff), instructional technology, academic computing, administrative computing, faculty members from a variety of disciplines, two library directors from other Rhode Island universities, a student representative, and the director of the University's Instructional Development Program.

The committee's first task was to propose a job description. The committee began with descriptions from committee members representing, respectively, libraries, computers, and media, describing how someone in that field might follow a career path (e.g., degrees, prior experience) that would make the person a likely candidate for our position. We listened carefully to the faculty members on the committee talk about their needs, current and anticipated, in libraries, computers, and media in order to think about what additional skills, background, and other qualities might be most helpful in this new position. The committee also had a helpful discussion regarding the different "cultures" of the professional groups most closely allied with the position.

Discussing the "cultures" of the various groups was a useful exercise. While the two prominent cultures–representing libraries and academic computing–each bring strengths to the combined enterprise, the contributions are, in fact, distinct. The culture of the Library (and librarianship) reflects, above all, order. Most institutions, ours included, hire librarians prepared in ALA accredited programs. While our librarians are appointed as faculty members, there is, within the Library, the habit of definite hours-per-week (a habit not replicated among faculty members in other units). Professional staff in the Academic Computer Center, on the other hand, come from a variety of professional preparations and described with some pride their willing ability to solve problems as they need to be solved, with substantially less regard to the hour, day, or week that the need arose. Librarians tended to see their problems as long-term, with staffing as regular within the week; computer staff tended to focus more on the great changes within their technology, the legitimate needs of their institution to have staff ensure that the technology is available to faculty and staff around the clock.

Clearly the differences between library and computer staff are due in large part to the histories of the two groups. Libraries, with a centuries-old tradition, developed their notions of essential tasks before significant computer technical support. Through its attention to cataloging–one of the great contributions of librarianship–although arguably its contemporary nemesis, librarianship has established itself as a field concerned fundamentally with order. In contrast, modern computing has developed within the lifespan of today's professionals. The power of computing has increased exponentially within the past three decades. Professionals in computing have been prepared in a relatively unordered array of degree programs. They have prided themselves on the essential creativity of their work. They have embraced, whether enthusiastically or through necessity, a dizzying array of changing technologies–along with the metaphors that describe them, the users that expect to rely on them, the prices needed to provide them, and the functions they can reliably support. Finding a way to search for and hire someone who could bridge and support these two cultures was a fundamental challenge for the committee.

The matter of required (or preferred) degrees was, perhaps understandably, a salient point of discussion for the committee. We concluded that a graduate degree was required and that a graduate degree related to the position (e.g., M.L.S. or Ph.D.) was preferred. In that parenthetical expression, each of the four elements was the subject of some discussion from varying points of view. Some–but not all–librarians felt strongly about requiring an M.L.S. for the head of the library; some–but not all–faculty members felt strongly about requiring a Ph.D. for a vice provostship. The degree choice was particularly important, given the University's Graduate School of Library and Information Studies. The committee had to balance the preference for an MLS degree for Library directors with the expectation among the teaching faculty of a Ph.D. for a Dean and Vice Provost. No quick answer is suggested, nor was one found. In the end the wording in the job announcement served us well, giving us a balance of focus and direction.

The salient features of the position are reproduced below:

VICE PROVOST AND DEAN OF UNIVERSITY LIBRARIES

Duties and Responsibilities. Responsible for planning, coordination and leadership of the University's academic information resources, including University Libraries, the Academic Computer Center, and the Audiovisual Center in support of the University's mission in instruction, research, and academic outreach. Assure a service orientation and coordination of campus resources, planned change, and continuous improvement. Lead the University Libraries and academic computing in cooperating with other Rhode Island and New England academic and research partners. The Vice Provost will report to the Provost and will be a member of the Provost's staff and the Council of Deans.

Required Qualifications. The successful candidate will demonstrate an understanding of the mission, role, and operations of libraries, academic computing, and information technologies, with significant prior experience in at least one of these areas; have a record of accomplishments sufficient for the position of vice provost/dean; demonstrate ability to further the goals of the library, computing, audiovisual technologies, and information technologies to support the teaching and research of the faculty and the learning outcomes of students; have five or more years of successful administrative experience in a complex environment; demonstrate excellent interpersonal and communication skills; and hold an advanced degree, preferably one relevant to the position (e.g., M.L.S., or Ph.D.).

In the ad, we also noted:

> This is a newly configured position, reflecting the University's commitment to the centrality of information and libraries to the fulfillment of its mission; the successful candidate will have the opportunity to help shape the agenda.

While the newly configured position was wending its way through the approval process (Provost, President, Board of Governors), the search committee worked to plan the advertising and recruitment strategies, to develop plans for review of candidates, and to outline the reference check and interview process.

SEARCHING AND SCREENING CANDIDATES

In searching vigorously for a strong pool of candidates, the committee set out to do just that: to search. The committee used ads, letters to peer institutions, electronic postings on listservs, recruitment at conferences, and word-of-mouth to attract a pool of well-qualified candidates. The ad included a WWW address for additional information, both because we wanted the widest possible knowledge of the opportunity and because (in the early months of 1995) we believed that being explicit in our ad that information which was available on the World Wide Web was a salient way to attract the interest of qualified candidates. Clearly, the expectation of e-mail contact, of finding us on the World Wide Web, and of the power of listservs to announce the position, was absolutely powerful. We searched at a moment in the history of technology when using these technologies for a position representing a range of technical interest represented a clear message that we understood the power of the technical presentation.

While a small number of institutions experimented in the 1980s with relationships between libraries and computers, at the time of our search, the common wisdom had not yet identified the combination as a durable path to coordination. Indeed, it seemed to us that the early combinations were based on the promise of technology, and the dissatisfaction with those combinations may have been because the promise was not fulfilled at that time. By the time our institution undertook our search, technology, and perhaps more importantly, our understanding of technology, had advanced to the point that we could combine libraries, computing, and technology to serve the academic mission of the institution. Clearly, at least the interest was there in the larger community. Our ad was picked up and reposted by a number of library-related lists, but also in some form by the Teaching-Learning-and-Technology Roundtable of the American Association of Higher Education, and by EDUCOM's Edupage list. Both of these latter lists have high visibility in academic administration and technology circles. Recruitment at conferences was also helpful, particularly at the ACRL meeting.

We attracted over 100 applicants, the vast majority of whom met the basic qualifications. Per our procedure, every member of the search committee was assigned to review every applicant, using a template that identified the required and preferred qualifications. From the 100+ applicants, and based on individual committee member review and our discussions, the committee identified about 16 candidates to pursue further. At this stage, successful administrative experience and indications that the person had solid experience in at least two of the three areas (libraries, academic computing [beyond the use of computers in libraries], and instructional technology) were particularly important. Also important was the communication, typically by the letter of application though also in some cases by the resume, that the candidate could address these three functions within the mission of our institution. A direct indication that the candidate knew how to work from the expressed need of the teaching and research faculty was also important. Arguably at least, compared with candidates for other dean/vice provost positions, the expectations for research and publication were reduced, while the expectations for a record of administrative impact were increased.

Each of these candidates was contacted by a member of the search committee who discussed the position, the institution, the progress of the search and the next steps. We contacted the three (or so) references submitted by each candidate, on a confidential basis, and based on the total information available, decided on a small number of people to bring to campus for interviews. The committee told each candidate at this stage that while our initial contact of references would be confidential, when we proceeded to the next step and a candidate agreed to come to campus, we assumed that the person's interest in our position was public information—and that we could call anyone we wished to at that point.

Based on candidate and reference telephone calls, we selected four people to come to campus for interviews.

CONCLUDING THE SEARCH

We were fortunate to have a strong pool of applicants and to invite four people to campus in whom we had confidence. Our confidence was not misplaced: we emerged from the interview process—and from the search process as a whole—believing that we could proceed to hire the candidate best for us at this time.

We learned more about our candidates, and hopefully hosted them more graciously by assigning an overall host to each candidate and four "half-day hosts" for the portions of the two-day interview. By spending two full days with each candidate, preceded by a dinner with representatives of the search committee, we worked to ensure that the search committee would get to know our candidates beyond the necessarily superficial impressions created in one-hour interview sessions.

Following the interviews, the search committee chair made up to nine additional telephone checks on each of the four candidates.

The information from the telephone reference calls, feedback forms from campus members who met each candidate, and the experience of search committee members was all used in a final meeting of the search committee. Each candidate was discussed, and based on all of the information available, a recommendation was made to the Provost consistent with our initial charge that we recommend at least three candidates. It can be safely noted that search committee members felt gratified with the interest in our position and with knowing that there was a pool of candidates who could undertake our position and move our agenda forward.

REFLECTIONS

Searches involve work and risk, both for institutions and candidates. With work and good luck, they can have outcomes beyond hiring a successful candidate. One invariably learns more than one set out to learn. Such is surely the case for the University of Rhode Island in this search, and we hope for many of our candidates as well. While the following observations cannot be documented sufficiently to satisfy research standards, they nonetheless represent important learning outcomes of the search process.

Successful searches typically have sufficient focus at the outset. The institution has a reasonably clear idea of the position and of the experience and qualifications of a successful candidate. To be sure, institutions learn about themselves and the position through the process of the search, but without sufficient focus before the search begins, the process can be unnecessarily frustrating for both the institution and the candidates.

It has become a cliché in libraryland to note the progression from focusing on collections to access. Indeed, as some writers have begun to observe, the next important focus is on use—and then on impact. Our search was helpful to us in making this transition. With no scientific evidence, but with the perspective of experience, it is likely that had we searched for a head of the library, we would have focused on access, with some attention to use. By considering the broader position of Vice Provost for [Academic] Information, we were forced to think about the use, and indeed the impact of the information from libraries, computing, and instructional technology—on the outcomes of our instruction, research, and academic outreach. Seldom, in any of these three realms (or most others within our institutions), does one focus so directly on the outcomes of one's investments.

Another cliché in libraryland, and the related portions of this position, is to focus on the service aspects of these functions. Clearly, libraries, academic computing, and instructional technology exist to help institutions fulfill the academic mission. There is no other rationale. Yet the ability to translate what one knows as an information professional to the day-to-day needs of faculty and students is not well developed. The ability to listen to faculty and to students talk about what they need in terms of information and technology support for their work is still limited.

Finally, while there is much rhetoric about the importance of connections between libraries, computing, and instructional technology, there are few examples indeed of integrating these units by learning how faculty use information resources in their teaching and research and then using that information to help structure services and outreach. Our leaders in these areas can help bring the power of technology to efficient use by the faculty and the academic administration. Providing this service will mean new organizational configurations and new deployment of talented staff. The leaders of today and tomorrow will value people's skills and contributions beyond the nomenclature of their degrees.

On a related point, the staff that support these functions will work to find new ways to relate to the teaching and research faculty. Talented staff in libraries, computers, and instructional technology can make powerful contributions to increasing the efficiency and effectiveness of teaching and research activities. Where use and impact are the goals, interaction with the faculty in their teaching and research are immeasurably more powerful than sitting with the faculty on routine committees.

Overall, the search committee was gratified by the large number of highly qualified candidates expressing an interest in the position. While we are gratified with our choice at hire, we are also gratified to know of the significant number of other qualified candidates, including but also extending beyond the people with whom we talked, who have developed and are developing the skills and perspectives to help lead the integration of academic information resources. Librarians fared well in our search. Our expectation is that with continuing changes in the field and individual initiative, they will continue to compete prominently for campus leadership positions.

CONCLUSION

In conclusion, our institution set out to search for a newly configured position, grappled with the differences in culture between librarians and computer professionals and worked with a relatively clear idea of what we needed to be successful, along with a shared commitment to attract a candidate who could provide vigorous leadership. The combination of searching and recruiting was essential and was well supported by a diverse and energetic search committee.

The Liberal Arts College Library Director and the Collegiate Myth

Joel Clemmer

INTRODUCTION

It is a supreme irony that an institution supported by such a significant body of literature can legitimately be described as "one of America's least examined, least understood institutions" but so it is with the liberal arts college.[1] The irony can be explained by a number of myths surrounding and supporting it. One can say "supporting" because, as in other contexts, myths can be essential to the success of the institution.

It is the intent of this paper to identify the perceived nature of the liberal arts college and to explore the meanings of these distinguishing characteristics for the library director. To identify these perceptions, an assessment on what teaching faculty have reported about the institutional environment will be made. In addition, faculty conclusions shall be compared to those made by college library directors. Besides reports in the literature, opinions were gathered from structured telephone interviews of nine college library directors who had assumed their positions within the last five years after significant experience in a contrasting work environment: that of the research university library. These directors are members of the

Joel Clemmer is Vice President for Library and Information Services, Macalester College, St. Paul, MN (e-mail: clemmer@macalstr.edu).

[Haworth co-indexing entry note]: "The Liberal Arts College Library Director and the Collegiate Myth." Clemmer, Joel. Co-published simultaneously in the *Journal of Library Administration* (The Haworth Press, Inc.) Vol. 24, No. 3, 1997, pp. 73-88; and: *The Academic Library Director: Reflections on a Position in Transition* (ed: Frank D'Andraia) The Haworth Press, Inc., 1997, pp. 73-88. Single or multiple copies of this article are available for a fee from The Haworth Document Delivery Service [1-800-342-9678, 9:00 a.m. - 5:00 p.m. (EST). E-mail address: getinfo@haworth.com].

Oberlin Group, an association of seventy-three selective liberal arts college libraries (see Appendix). The surveyed directors were asked to comment on their expectations upon assuming the liberal arts college directorship, what they most value and most dislike about the position and what skills their university experience afforded them that they otherwise may not have attained. The survey results, in addition to data collected from the literature, will be assessed to identify that which is perceived to be essential to the working environment of the private liberal arts college library director.

THE ESSENTIAL LIBERAL ARTS COLLEGE

The phrase "liberal arts college" itself is ambiguous. To define the set of institutions to be discussed, the statistical approach used by the Carnegie Foundation for the Advance of Teaching was selected. From this list were culled primarily undergraduate private institutions that award more than 50 percent of their baccalaureate degrees in the liberal arts.[2] Of the resulting 540 colleges, the Foundation finds 140 to be sufficiently selective to be ranked "liberal arts I," with the remaining 400 "liberal arts II." The label "liberal arts," however, came under scrutiny even following an earlier survey in 1976. It was accused of masking the fact that only one in five "liberal arts II" schools award at least 80 percent of their degrees in "classic academic fields" thus calling into question whether "liberal arts" retains meaning as distinct from professional or vocational education.[3] Similarly, David Breneman points out that if "liberal arts" connotes private schools awarding fewer than 25 percent of their degrees in preprofessional fields, then the 540 liberal arts colleges of the 1987 survey drops to 90, a very significant difference.[4] Breneman's core liberal arts schools have the common profile of supporting full time residential students of ages 18 through 24, numbering fewer than 2,500, and pursuing a selection of 20 to 24 majors, signified by baccalaureate degrees with virtually no undergraduate professional education.[5] An even more restrictive number was derived in the mid-1980s by an influential study of undergraduate colleges that produce a high proportion of science graduate students. The study identified 48 such schools, called "research colleges," which form the core of the Oberlin Group of libraries.[6] Thus, if measures of selectivity and curricular consistency are introduced, the end product is a set of fifty to one hundred such institutions in the U.S.

Yet, the numbers do not tell the really significant part of the story. The idea and image of the liberal arts college exercise an influence way out of proportion to its demographic. In a typical recitation of the emotions evoked by the institution, Kenyon alumnus P.F. Kluge notes that 80 percent of U.S. college students attend public institutions but

> When you picture a college, you see a place like Kenyon. For here in Gambier, Ohio, is the very image of a college–the college of memory and dream, out of Hollywood movies and Plato's cave, a college that is a confluence of people and place, of character and fate, architecture and landscape, college as a personal style, a way of life, college as a place where history matters and people remember, an island in space and time. Also, my alma mater.[7]

The themes of this effusive passage–the past as present, image as perceived reality, the college as historical community, the importance of collective persona in a close community–also turn out to be drivers in librarians' responses to the liberal arts college, in part because academic librarians share the myths of their culture and in part as outcomes of their work experience.

The intense relationship of the individual to the collegiate community is among the core values of the institution and one which this paper explores from the librarians' perspective. It is an outcome of the earliest antecedents of U.S. higher education. It was not until 1876 that Johns Hopkins grafted the German ideal of research onto the Anglo-American approach to undergraduate education, producing a multiplication of academic departments, elective courses and specializations, the culmination of which is the modern research university.[8] During this period of change in the late nineteenth century, the private liberal arts college developed a romantic interpretation of its status as a community of learning, often set apart in a small town and offering the individual an intense relationship with a small, supportive institution. The richness of its symbolic life and "organizational saga" became crucial to ongoing support, actually making the college seem more like an intense community than an organization.[9] This romantic view of community in the liberal arts college remains crucial to its attractiveness, a fact proven by perpetual fears of its decline (Hayford 1990, 3).[10] The dichotomy of community and organization is another theme which we will examine from the librarian's perspective.

Eminent commentators such as the late Ernest Boyer have supported the liberal arts college and its curriculum as a bulwark against a creeping market orientation in education with its business and professional values, usually embodied by preprofessional and graduate courses.[11] Curricular purity is often packaged with community values in defining the essential liberal arts college. As a context for exploring librarians' reaction to it, it is possible to deconstruct this ideal type to reveal the unconscious transcendent ideas, rhetorical claims and binary distinctions on which it is based. An examination of recent, influential survey reports on higher education by the National Institute of Education, the National Endowment for the Humanities, the Association of American Colleges and the Carnegie Foundation found the survey reports to be "steeped in the beliefs and conceptions associated with the pre-Civil War liberal arts college" and continuing as a basis of belief in the superiority of today's private liberal arts college.[12] The favorable assumptions embodied in words such as "small," "private," "teaching," "undergraduate," "liberal" (as opposed to occupational) seem to influence value choices in general educational policy and, not coincidentally, lend a positive aura to the educational institution that most clearly exhibits them. To the extent that this prejudicial vocabulary also includes a romantic rejection of "business philosophy and values" in education, these are some interesting issues to explore in library and collegiate administration.[13]

Liberal arts colleges, when closely defined, constitute a very small territory in the landscape of higher education yet represent a transcendent educational ideal that may be based more on myth than fact. The private liberal arts college embodies a set of values presumed to constitute a superior educational environment. Whether that useful myth translates into an advantaged working environment for the college library director is our next question.

UNIVERSITIES AND COLLEGES

One way to gain perspective on the question is to contrast the working environment of the college with that of the university. The literature describing library directors at the research university level tends toward the pessimistic. More than twenty years ago, it was reported that more than half of the A.R.L. directorships had changed in a three year period.[14] The trend continues with Woodsworth's report from the late '80s of retrenchment, university administrative turnover and lack of management experience, growing layers of administrative overhead, budget crises and so on.[15] Few escape routes are available to the harried research librarian who does not have recourse to a teaching position. Among them, Woodsworth identified moving to "smaller, single purpose institutions where library goals are achievable."[16] In fact, there seems to be an increasingly well trodden path leading from research libraries to those of private liberal arts colleges. Of the sixteen Oberlin Group library directors who have assumed their positions in the last five years and for whom information was available, nine have recent experience in research libraries.

Do liberal arts colleges fulfill the high expectations? From the faculty and administrators' point of view, the answer is "generally yes." Investigators with the U.C.L.A. Study of the Academic Profession conducted hundreds of interviews in nine institutional types between 1983 and 1985 and concluded that basic satisfaction was highest in liberal arts colleges. Fifty six percent of faculty in Carnegie Category I colleges agreed that their college "is a very good place for me."[17] Job satisfaction surveys show higher levels of overall satisfaction among librarians of smaller academic libraries.[18] Chapin and Hardesty found little of the intra-institutional conflict Woodsworth claimed was typical of large universities when they surveyed liberal arts library directors and deans. In fact, they found that the liberal arts college library was often afforded privileged budgetary status.[19]

Accordingly, the Oberlin Group interviewees had high expectations upon moving to the liberal arts college directorship. Most anticipated relief from the management difficulties of large institutions, an intimate work environment in which one can deal with the major players on a face to face basis, and more involvement in the teaching learning process, including closer contact with faculty and students. With few exceptions, these expectations seem to have been met and provided a very satisfactory work experience. Speaking in the comparative sense, one director with university experience said, "Life is quite sweet in these institutions." Negative expectations logically included the lack of comparable resources and, in addition, frequent mention was made of separation from the larger world of librarianship. There was an expectation (borne out by experience) that leaving behind the cutting edge projects, promotion requirements and other inducements to "get out there" would lead to a feeling of separation from the field at large. Likewise, some directors regretted leaving behind the "world class" collections, graduate students and advanced programs of their former institutions.

This set of expectational pluses and minuses is confirmed by analogy on the faculty side. Clark found that faculty at research institutions expressed positive aspects of their experience in terms of "first rateness" of scholarship, research and colleagues, and are more oriented to people and events outside the institution. Liberal arts college faculty, in contrast, speak first of their close association with students, friendship and collaboration with local colleagues and the ethos of teaching in an often beautiful setting.[20] Overall, liberal arts college faculty are said to give priority to their college community over the scholarly discipline, compared with research institution faculty.[21,22] The expectations of the Oberlin Group interviewees on this score were borne out by a study of time allocation of liberal arts college library directors versus those of research institutions. The former were found to spend more time on their internal library roles than external activities.[23]

COMMUNITY IN THE LIBERAL ARTS COLLEGE

The values of community often came up in the Oberlin Group interviews, both quantitatively in terms of sheer size of the organization and qualitatively in terms of the nature of relationships within it. These played out in replies to the question of what the interviewees most value in their current college work environment. Three categories appeared: the value of nonbureaucratic working relationships in a college; the ability to have an institution-wide impact and the relative ease of getting things done compared with a university. The first set of replies signifies the face to face nature of collegiate working relationships without the hindrances of intervening offices and paper. In the words of one respondent, "I can be more myself and manage based on who I am as a person instead of on a symbolic plane." Consequently, responses tend to be faster in the collegiate organization and support for library tasks is quicker to arrive. It was also pointed out that things happened more quickly because, in the smaller community, the players attribute a higher level of competence to each other based on familiarity and are less likely to depend on an institutional imprimatur. Indeed, Chapin and Hardesty report that the characteristic of the library director most valued by liberal arts college deans is "interpersonal skills"—the ability to communicate successfully with faculty, students, staff and the administration.[24] While there were some references among librarians to shared institutional goals, most reports in this category were either at the level of personal working relationships or simply getting things done in the smaller community.

The Oberlin Group interviewees also spoke of the relative freedom they enjoyed to initiate projects and get them going. This is an operational outcome of community characteristics already mentioned. Discussion pointed out, in addition, their direct access to decision makers and relative absence of institutional turf battles compared with their experience in universities. In these characteristics, confirmed by survey research of liberal arts faculty, the group reported being reasonably comfortable with their shared authority with and direct access to the administration.[25] In the smaller institution, "the administration can't hide" says one faculty respondent. Many Oberlin Group interviewees report relief at not having to navigate such treacherous bureaucratic waters, and theories abound about what factors, other than sheer size, play a role. This discussion was usually preceded with acknowledgment of the limited resources of the liberal arts college.

Research based on other segments of academic institutions casts light on and generally supports librarians' reports of community characteristics. The expectation of greater institution-wide impact in the small college is reasonable, according to reported perceptions of the university. Descriptions of the university by faculty are more likely to be about their own unit, compared with liberal arts college faculty.[26] The whole is inferred from the part and the image that emerges is close to Clark Kerr's famous line describing the multiversity as a federation of departments united only by the heating plant. Likewise, "community" in the university context often refers to the disciplinary community, one of physical dispersal but shared intellectual interests.[27] The coin of this realm is the "first rateness" mentioned earlier–the sense of being in the academic vanguard.

While the collegiate community as a set of personal relationships affords opportunities for satisfaction, there are reported down sides as well. A fired college library director reports that a major obstacle to success was the fact that small colleges strongly reflect their regional and ethnic cultures and also their own social histories, as opposed to the more cosmopolitan large university. Failure to deal successfully with such cultural variables can stop a career.[28] While the Oberlin Group interviewees had no such extreme results to report, there were some problems with the ideal of close, harmonious community in the liberal arts college. In the words of one, "These institutions are very touchy," meaning that a complaint by a single student can haunt the manager. More than one respondent noted that, counter to the notion of intimate participation in the undergraduate teaching learning process, the absence of graduate programs actually worked to separate librarians from students. In the university, the graduate students are often among the hungriest for collaboration with librarians. The fact that many new Oberlin Group directors work the reference desk provides only fleeting participation in the educational process though the total time spent with students may be significant.[29] It was also noted that face to face problem solving in the college has a flip side: issues are often personalized. While this hardly is unique to smaller institutions, the fact of smallness reportedly makes it more blatant and hard to avoid. Finally, the respondents reported in many contexts an ironic sense of personal isolation in the midst of their otherwise close community. Factors here include the fact that university library directors have a multifaceted institution within which to find personal and professional companionship. "Universities support a larger number of departments, programs and research institutes, all of which have directors who face management problems similar to that of the library director," according to one interviewee. There is a potential network here which is much larger than that typically available to the collegiate director. Another factor is the geographic isolation of many liberal arts schools, a heritage of the presumptions of their founding discussed earlier. "There is only one of me," was repeated in the interviews.

It seems that both liberal arts colleges and research universities support a notion of community but the definitions differ. In other words, both have a definable character to which one can relate one's own set of preferences. In this, they share a characteristic and, together, differ from educational institutions in the ranks of lesser known universities and comprehensive colleges. These often have more of a challenge forging their institutional self definition and do not support such a clear institutional culture.[30] It is possible that the presence of a clear institutional personality, complete with the "organizational sagas" depicted earlier, affords opportunity for satisfaction in the form of a context within which one can operate subject to known and predictable parameters.

THREATS TO THE COLLEGIATE COMMUNITY

As mentioned above, published reports express a fear of compromising the special characteristics of the liberal arts college which could change this favorable picture. The chief academic officers of the Associated Colleges of the Midwest have expressed a concern that the collegiate community of the past, based on undergraduate teaching, may be subverted by a newly rigorous, publication driven agenda which would detract from teaching and redirect the faculty's energies off campus.[31] Robert D. Stueart voiced precisely the same concern about the college librarian when he observed that promotion and tenure requirements in liberal arts colleges are growing closer to those of research universities, creating a distracting pressure on librarians.[32]

When one confines one's view to the so called "top fifty liberal arts colleges," there is reportedly competition with research universities for the same faculty, leading to the surmise that the research driven agenda is finding its way into undergraduate teaching.[33] Kluge reports that a generational turnover among faculty is changing the personality of his alma mater, turning the small college into a "larger place."[34] The sense of campus community at the more ambitious liberal arts colleges thus could be threatened by the more remote "community of academic discipline."[35] On the library side, Evan Farber of Earlham College detected a "university library syndrome" among college faculty, administrators and librarians that led to evaluating the library in terms of size instead of service, to pursuit of research materials instead of those appropriate to undergraduates and to undervaluing librarians as faculty colleagues.[36]

RESEARCH AND THE COLLEGE

Within the profession itself, Farber notes the tendency of university trained librarians to import the values of the research agenda to the college and of university librarians to dominate through professional activities.[37] The sources researched for this paper confirm only one of these two assertions. The literature and the interviews of recently appointed Oberlin Group directors confirm that national visibility is more accessible to librarians at research institutions and they are more often prompted to seek out activities which provide it. The supposed phenomenon of librarians carrying a research agenda into the liberal arts college from their university training grounds is more questionable. More than one interviewee did express regret leaving behind the "world class" collections of their former institutions. As it happens, though, they found themselves in a college library supporting unique special collections and identified those as an outlet. The very emphasis on having made a transition, however, points out a recognition of the distinct emphasis on undergraduate teaching in the liberal arts college. More interviewees spoke of moving to the liberal arts college precisely as a remedy for the perceived separation from the teaching learning process. Typically, they reported that faculty proposed to acquire research materials but quickly backed off when the distinction between these and material appropriate to undergraduates was explained. There was relatively little conflict over building research collections reported by this set of librarians.

The broader issue of research in the liberal arts college is important, however, and the terms of the debate affect liberal arts college library directors. As background, one could note that the doing of research ranks high in the hierarchy of faculty tasks but may be more honored in the breach in the average four-year institution. Twenty seven percent of faculty in liberal arts I colleges have never published an article and 38 percent have not published one in the preceding two years.[38] It is potentially true, however, that the extent to which a research agenda is brought to the liberal arts college unchanged from its home at the research institutions may compromise the undergraduate, teaching and communal ideals of the college. Part and parcel of the former is an orientation to the scholarly community outside the college and intellectual activity at a level beyond that attainable by most undergraduates.[39] In terms of collection building and other programmatic support, this would be a nearly impossible agenda for the liberal arts college library to pursue at the level attained by research libraries.

There turns out to be evidence that the nature of research among liberal arts faculty differs from that practiced by university faculty and that the former is, unsurprisingly, better adapted to the collegiate environment. Liberal arts college faculty are more likely to justify research as an investment in students and to shape research projects as a way to expose students to a variety of ideas and subjects.[40] Their projects are more likely to cut across subdisciplinary boundaries to be less dependent on large scale bureaucratic support. In general, liberal arts faculty research tends to have "horizontal" taxonomy and to take advantage of the accessibility of faculty colleagues in other fields.[41] It is thus more closely tied to the teaching goal of the liberal arts college.

This evidence may have a partial resolution of the difficulty of interpreting faculty expectations in the liberal arts environment. The evidence leads us to avoid dealing with "research" as a generality and to ask what sort of needs are engendered by particular projects. Those undertaken by liberal arts faculty may be more closely aligned with the goals and resources of the college library than many of us assume.

THE COLLEGE AS MANAGED ORGANIZATION

The beginning of this paper discussed a potential conflict between the liberal arts college as a community of personalized relationships and the college as a managed organization. This is another tension that is visible in both the literature and in interviews with Oberlin Group directors. In the article "After the fall: reflections on being fired," the anonymous author named "lack of management training" among the chief causes of failure.[42] The theory here is that university librarians get management experience and training as they advance through rank while small college librarians may find themselves suddenly off the front lines and in the manager's office. The typical educational background of academic librarians fails to compensate for this difference because it is so highly concentrated in certain disciplines, none of them managerial by one researcher's definition. Sixty percent of academic librarians' undergraduate degrees are in four disciplines, 45 percent of the total in history or English alone. These two subjects accounted for 35 percent of second Master's degrees as well.[43] Quantitative and technical disciplines are generally lacking.

Within this issue lurk unclear definitions on what is meant by "management" and the role of administrative control in the college overall. Two themes emerge in the literature to help with the definitional problem. When enumerating specific problems faced in his or her college experience, the anonymous author lists "bringing people along with change; gaining trust; and winning cooperation"–hardly issues unique to the liberal arts college.[44] In fact, testimony quoted so far seems to suggest opportunities within the distinctive set of close, personalized working relationships of the college to deliver just such advocacy. The issue here may be another instance of the difficulty of operating within the narrow limits of cultural acceptance in a small community.

The issue of technical managerial preparation for the college library directorship is also a challenge. Chapin and Hardesty found little support for the notion that contemporary collegiate administration belongs to zealous bureaucrats "learned in such matters as program budgeting, decision matrices and cost benefit analysis." Indeed, they found that most academic deans collect evaluative library data based on casual observation and comparisons with other institutions and with a minimum of statistics.[45] Even the recently retired Dean of Arts and Sciences at Harvard reports that "most plans and studies yielded obvious results that were already in my head by way of intuition." According to Henry Rosovsky, it is the university president, acting from an "Olympian perspective," who demands such data.[46]

These sentiments may be as expressive of the cultural history of colleges and universities as they are of real management needs. Academia has been depicted as a quiet battleground between competing conceptions of authority. The rise of faculty control over the newly complex curriculum in the nineteenth century was bolstered by the ethos of the "scholarly guild," an essentially antibureaucratic set of assumptions valuing instead expertise within the discipline. It had to find a way to coexist with the more traditional hierarchically managed style already developed by the university president and his administration.[47] The potential for conflict between the two is greatest at institutions that depend most on supporting advanced scholarship by faculty, an activity linked closely to the antimanagerial values of the scholarly guild. The institutions where the contrast is most stark are the more prestigious universities and colleges. "The higher the standing of the university or college, the more likely it is to avoid the trappings of strict managerialism."[48]

A similar conclusion is reached via the deconstructionist route when Rhoades finds that educational assumptions in the United States are under the sway of a preindustrial model which reaches its zenith in selective, private institutions. Here, he finds a "devaluation of all things related to private enterprise" and/or the "practical, useful and specialized."[49] Since, in the same set of institutions, other observers have noted frequent transitions between the administrative suites and faculty positions, it is not surprising that college administrators, in particular, express ambivalence about the trappings of managerialism. Indeed, the potential conflict between the two camps is solved by ambiguity, what one commentator calls "delicate fictions, ambiguous definitions—and patience."[50]

It is not surprising that recently appointed liberal arts college library directors who were contacted identified many management skills they had to develop in the university environment which they feel they would not have had they spent their careers in liberal arts colleges. The most commonly cited was the management of people, expressed as knowing the value of rigorous personnel policies, "people management," and participatory management. There was also frequent mention of the need to "present plans in public in a way that people can relate to them." This represents a change from the previously reported inward orientation of college library directors and, since it was often expressed in terms of plans for technology, may represent a new trend in their work life.

When challenged to name the principal differences between their current liberal arts college experience and that in larger institutions, the interviewees optimistically replied "more engaging," "intimacy," "simplicity," "easier to get things done," "I miss the world class collection," "cross functional flexibility," "the community is too touchy," or "more fun." In short, a somewhat mixed but generally favorable array.

CONCLUSION

The liberal arts college is an ideal with ideational power beyond its actual numbers. Essential to this power is the emotive vision of an academic community, its implicit reference to preindustrial and antimanagerial stereotypes and perceived relief from bureaucracy. These notions are confirmed by the literature and testimony of recently appointed Oberlin Group librarians who previously worked in research university libraries.

The information sources offer congruent descriptions of the working environment of the college library director. The positive expectations of personalized working relationships, responsive support apparatus, and likelihood of institution wide influence usually are met. Negative experiences of isolation from the perceived cutting edge of the field, a more inward focus and constricting local culture are widely shared. The positives and negatives have analogies in the reported experience of teaching faculty. The ideal of close contact with teaching faculty and students is inconsistently fulfilled. Research and organizational managerialism are accommodated by the college with difficulty.

Directing the liberal arts college library can provide much personal satisfaction but requires understanding of the peculiar working environment of the college as an institutional type.

NOTES

1. Paul Frederick Kluge, *Alma Mater: A College Homecoming* (Reading, MA: Addison Wesley, 1993), 12.

2. Carnegie Foundation for the Advancement of Teaching, *A Classification of Institutions of Higher Education* (Princeton: The Foundation, 1987), 7.

3. Raymond F. Zammuto, "Are the Liberal Arts an Endangered Species?" *Journal of Higher Education* 55, no. 2 (1984): 21.

4. David W. Breneman, *Liberal Arts Colleges: Thriving, Surviving or Endangered?* (Washington, DC: Brookings Institute, 1994), 12.

5. Ibid.

6. David Davis-Van Atta, "The Future of Science at Liberal Arts Colleges," in *Educating America's Scientist: The Role of the Research College: A Report for the Conference held at Oberlin College, Oberlin, Ohio 9-10 June 1985* (Oberlin, Ohio: Office of the Provost, Oberlin College, 1985).

7. Kluge, 2.

8. Francis Oakley, *Community of Leaning: The American College and the Liberal Tradition* (New York: Oxford, 1992), 62.

9. Burton R. Clark, *The Academic Life: Small Worlds; Different Worlds* (Princeton: The Carnegie Foundation for the Advancement Teaching, 1987), 7.

10. Elizabeth R. Hayford, "Intellectual Community in Liberal Arts Colleges," *Liberal Education* 76, no. 5 (1990): 3.

11. Ernest L. Boyer, *College: The Undergraduate Experience in America* (New York: Harper & Row, 1987), XIII.

12. Gary Rhoades, "Calling on the Past: The Quest for the Collegiate Ideal," *Journal of Higher Education* 61, no. 5 (1990): 529.

13. Ibid., 531.

14. Arthur M. McAnally and Robert B. Downs, "The Changing Role of Directors of University Libraries," *College & Research Libraries* 34, no. 2 (1973): 103-125.

15. Anne Woodsworth, "Getting off the Merry-go-round: McAnally and Downs Revisited," *Library Journal* 114, no. 6 (1989): 35-38.

16. Ibid., 38.

17. Clark, 220.

18. Mohammad Mirfakhari, "Correlates of Job Satisfaction Among Academic Libraries in the United States," *Journal of Library Administration* 14, no. 1 (1991): 117-131.

19. Lloyd W. Chapin and Larry Hardesty, "Benign Neglect of the "Heart of the College:" Liberal Arts College Deans Look at the Library," in *Academic Libraries: Their Rationale and Role in American Higher Education,* ed. Gerard B. McCabe and Ruth J. Person (Westport, CT: Greenwood, 1995), 29-41.

20. Clark, 112.

21. Michael Nelson, "Faculty and Community in the Liberal Arts College (with observations on research and teaching)," *Politics Science and Politics* 27, no. 1 (1994): 73-76.

22. Ernest L. Boyer, *Scholarship Reconsidered: Priorities of the Professorate* (Princeton: Carnegie Foundation for the Advancement of Teaching, 1990).

23. Terence F. Mech, "Academic Library Directors: A Managerial Role Profile," *College & Research Libraries* 51, no. 5 (1994): 415-427.

24. Chapin and Hardesty, 34.

25. Clark, 162.

26. Ibid., 110.

27. Nelson, 73.

28. Anonymous, "After the fall: Reflections on Being Fired," *Journal of Academic Librarianship* 17, no. 5 (1991): 302-303.

29. Mech, 425.

30. Clark, 114.

31. Hayford, 4.

32. Robert D. Stueart, "The Liberal Arts College Library: Paradox or Panacea?" *College & Research Libraries* 51, no. 6 (1990), 524-529.

33. Henry Rosovsky, *The University: An Owner's Manual* (New York: W. W. Norton, 1990), 81.

34. Kluge, 22.

35. Nelson 73.

36. Evan Ira Farber, "College Librarians and the University-Library Syndrome" in *The Academic Library: Essays in Honor of Guy R. Lyle* ed. Evan Ira Farber and Ruth Walling (Metuchen, NJ: Scarecrow, 1974).

37. Ibid., 18.

38. Boyer, *Scholarship Reconsidered: Priorities of the Professorate,* xvii.

39. Nelson, 74.

40. Kenneth Ruscio, "The Distinctive Scholarship of the Selective Liberal Arts College," *Journal of Higher Education* 58, no. 2 (1987): 205-222.

41. Ibid., 214.

42. Anonymous, 302.

43. Mark E. Cain, "Academic and Research Librarians: Who Are We?" *Journal of Academic Librarianship* 14, no. 5 (1988): 292-296.

44. Anonymous, 302.

45. Chapin and Hardesty, 32.

46. Rosovsky, 46.

47. Clark, 150.

48. Theodore Caplow and Reece J. McGee, *The Academic Marketplace* (New York: Basic Books, 1958), 152.

49. Rhoades, 530.

50. Clark, 150.

Director's Challenge:
Academic Libraries, Risky Business
or a Business at Risk?

Frank D'Andraia

Every decade has its issues. In the 1990s the paramount issue for higher education administrators, such as academic library directors, has been the struggle to maintain and expand services in a climate where traditional sources of funding are continuously threatened and where new revenue sources are hotly contested. Many believe that in order to maintain, adjust, and prosper, academic library directors, as well as other campus administrators, need to move forward as other consumer industries have and reinvent their organizations. To many outside of academia, particularly state legislators, the perception is growing that higher education hasn't learned from the changes that have affected other consumer industries such as the automobile and steel industries, who have coped with market competition; airlines and railroads, who have dealt with changing consumer demands; and banks and Baby Bells who have shed workers because of technological efficiencies. In the coming decade many see the number one issue confronting campus administrators to be how higher education, a "not-for-profit" culture, successfully embraces "for-profit" principles.

Frank D'Andraia is Director of Libraries, University of North Dakota, Grand Forks, ND (e-mail: dandraia@plains.nodak.edu).

[Haworth co-indexing entry note]: "Director's Challenge: Academic Libraries, Risky Business or a Business at Risk?" D'Andraia, Frank. Co-published simultaneously in the *Journal of Library Administration* (The Haworth Press, Inc.) Vol. 24, No. 3, 1997, pp. 89-100; and: *The Academic Library Director: Reflections on a Position in Transition* (ed: Frank D'Andraia) The Haworth Press, Inc., 1997, pp. 89-100. Single or multiple copies of this article are available for a fee from The Haworth Document Delivery Service [1-800-342-9678, 9:00 a.m. - 5:00 p.m. (EST). E-mail address: getinfo@haworth.com].

JOBS DISAPPEAR AND CHANGE IN EVERY AGE

Jobs disappear and change in any age. What distinguishes these times from past periods of transformation is the depth, breadth, and speed of today's changing nature of work. No sector of the nation's workforce appears to be exempt. This pattern and cycle may have occurred first in smoke stack industries, such as steel, auto, and rails, but by the 1990s jobs began to disappear and change shape in smoke free corporations, such as finance, telecommunications, and electronics. The change process has been wrenching for both blue and white collar workers. As the decade of the 1990s comes to a close, operations like higher education are poised to experience the same employee dislocation and organizational redesign as their counterparts in the profit motivated sector.

FACTORS DRIVING JOB CHANGE AND REDESIGN

There are many factors driving the redesign of jobs, chief among which is the impact of new technology that "lets machines replace hands and minds,"[1] a phrase which raises the hackles of academic library personnel, but which in large measure cannot be denied. Other factors include increasing competition, changing societal needs, and exacting demands for greater economies.[2] Academia faces many of the same issues that confronted big business in the 1980s. From the post World War II years forward, higher education repeatedly responded to consumer growth by expanding programs, constructing or enlarging campuses, and demanding and obtaining greater federal and state support. For example, during the postwar years California built more than 42 community colleges, four new California State University (CSU) campuses and three new branch campuses of the University of California (UC).[3]

Like bank branch expansion in the 1980s, the growth of campuses was intended to address the needs of the baby boomers of the 1960s and 1970s. But also like the banking boom of the 1980s, the overbuilding and expansion weakened the long-term health of higher education. By the time the baby boom had subsided, higher education was left with overcapacity in facilities and faculty, falling revenues and rising fixed costs, new consumer demands and escalating competition for new students.[4-7]

EVOLVING NEEDS
OF HIGHER EDUCATION CONSUMERS

The future needs of college consumers are significantly different from past generations. Today's college age student is more likely to be nonwhite, older, a part-timer, a parent, or "determinedly job oriented."[8] Thanks to technology bringing the classroom into the living room, a growing number of students are electing to take their classes at home, far removed from a central campus. Moreover, this new wave of students is not expected to inundate the nation uniformly. Student growth rates will be strongest in the West, followed by the South, Northeast, and Midwest regions.[9,10]

Today's knowledge society generation has expectations that are significantly different from past generations. The students of the 1990s fully grasp the power they possess as consumers in the education marketplace. As consumers, they expect the academy to tailor courses to demand, embrace new approaches to teaching, and initiate programs and services that are consumer sensitive and not tradition bound.[11,12]

CHANGING ATTITUDES
OF HIGHER EDUCATION ADVOCATES

The attitudes of those who underwrite higher education operations have also changed. Voters have begun to support caps on higher education spending. Legislatures, especially those located in the western states that form the Western Governors Conference, are demanding that the people's money be spent more selectively. Solons are requiring that technological options be explored in lieu of expanding existing institutions, constructing new campuses, hiring new faculty, and building more libraries. Politicians are looking for new cost-effective vehicles to deliver education. An example of new alternatives to standard educational models is the Western

Governors University in which students can earn academic certification and even degrees by taking classes over the Internet or through video uplinks. Other new options include "for-profit" operations such as National University and the growing commitment by many traditionally structured institutions to provide distance learning education.[13],[14]

OLD SOLUTIONS FOR NEW CHALLENGES

Today's college consumers may have new expectations about higher education and may influence some who teach and operate the nation's campuses. However, many faculty continue to cling tenaciously to values, aspirations, and attitudes that are at odds with evolving educational trends on such topics as distance learning, electronic document delivery, and tenure. The higher education industry lacks discipline to change because unlike other consumer organizations, it has not been recently tested. In years past academy issues and strategies focused on hiring eminent faculty, creating notable libraries, constructing new labs, producing great athletic teams, and developing traditions of excellence. Colleges and universities, as "not-for-profit" enterprises, and in many cases state assisted operations, were often sheltered from the business realities that forced other consumer driven enterprises to change and adapt. When occasional economies were required, for example, many schools commissioned new recruiting packages designed to attract more students. Other institutions developed new marketing concepts and initiated capital campaigns. Concomitantly, spending on laboratories, physical plants, equipment, and libraries were temporarily curtailed. Staffing levels for support operations were momentarily trimmed. While these efforts abruptly generated income and economies, they do not produce the needed revenues required to sustain long-term viability, underwrite significant change or address the crucial issue of replacing falling federal and state support.[15]

"NOT-FOR-PROFIT"
DOES NOT MEAN OPERATING AT A LOSS

Today, many higher education institutions exhibit a newfound fiscal conservatism. In Boston's Fenway district, for example, several area colleges are proposing to consolidate similar operations, such as food services and security, with neighboring institutions to reduce costs.[16] Nationwide academic libraries have closed branches, contracted out some technical activities, and reduced the need to annually commit millions of dollars to renew costly and infrequently used journals. Higher education administrators are rapidly becoming sensitive to the fact that while their institution may have "not-for-profit" status, this does not give them license to operate at a loss.

Yet, considerable resistance has developed when campus administrators attempt to address one of the highest cost centers in any enterprise: wages. According to a recent article in *Fortune*, college and university salaries and benefits account for about 50 percent of spending at institutions with medical schools and research programs. Campus labor expenses are reported to be even higher at liberal arts colleges.[17]

Occasionally some university president attempts to trim faculty size and administrative ranks. This action has met with significant resistance to date. For example, former Yale President Benno Smith announced in 1992 his intention to close a big budget gap in the arts and sciences by cutting programs and departments. That ignited a faculty revolt that soon led to his departure. At California State University (CSU), San Diego and at the City University New York (CUNY), campus presidents have made significant pronouncements concerning faculty positions, only to defer or alter original proposals.[18]

While internal efforts to significantly streamline and restructure operations and resources are rejected, external pressures from trustees, regents, and boards of higher education are increasing. These various boards of overseers are demanding more rigorous fiscal accountability, higher levels of productivity and greater degrees of economy. The regents of the University of Minnesota (UM) have, for example, proposed a new form of tenure that allows for greater flexibility in the hiring and retention of non-union faculty.[19] Non-unionist UM faculty overwhelmingly rejected the proposed changes.[20] At the University of Rochester, proposals to downsize the number of graduate programs and shrink the size of the faculty have been rebuffed by faculty.[21] Indeed, faculty have countered with a familiar refrain. They are demanding campus officials address the issue of administrative overhead.[22]

THE BUSINESS MODEL

Legislators in particular have helped drive home the message that a businesslike approach to higher education operations is a laudable goal and a high priority. In North Dakota, for example, the Governor has demanded that the North Dakota University System review tenure, restructure operations, reallocate resources, and increase collaborative ventures before any consideration of additional financial support is made.[23]

Clearly, the pressure is building on higher education to deal with the fixed cost centers of salaries and benefits. The model often used as an example of success is the model developed by the business sector. The focal points of the business model include downsizing staff, job redesign, and operational restructuring. When applied to academia, the business model calls for revising tenure, streamlining operations, and reducing administrative and faculty positions.[24] The business model demands for a total revamping of "Byzantine" policies and practices affecting campus teaching, operations, and services.[25]

While campus administrators, faculty, regents, and legislators duke it out over the issue of tenure, campus service units such as the library do not have the luxury of postponing action. In past campus crises, libraries have always been vulnerable when costs and resources have become tight. Often campus administrators have unilaterally and presumptuously required the library to reduce costs, freeze appointments, suspend acquisitions, and make other economies in order to assist in controlling campus costs without time for planning or regard to effect. As campus costs continue to rise and revenues continue to lag, library administrators no doubt will be targeted for greater economies.

To date, academic library administrators have had some success in achieving these economies and justifying their programs by bidding contracts, collaborating in the development of statewide networks, finding new alternatives to comprehensive print-based collection building, developing new revenue streams, and contracting out selective operations and services. Moreover, libraries use their electronic management report systems, as well as data provided by vendors, to help them better track costs, services, and revenues. Online public access catalogs generate considerable amounts of management information allowing administrators to track key library activities, including building use and revenues (overdues, fines, interlibrary charges). Software has been available for years to help libraries track and analyze historical use patterns concerning collections and borrowers. In recent years libraries have begun to install software to track photocopying, CD use and other services. While the technology has let library administrators squeeze a little more juice from the orange, the larger issue of vulnerability as an institution at risk is yet to be addressed.

PAY AND PERFORMANCE AND "NOT-FOR-PROFIT" CULTURE

The business sector has found performance-based pay to be an effective way to economize and address the organizational changes that have occurred because of job redesign and downsizing. The concept is simple: people who perform at a higher level should be paid more than those whose perform at a lower level. The concept is appealing to business for several reasons. It fits corporate culture, it emphasizes competition, performance, success, and reward. Performance-based pay is designed to retain the most valuable and productive employees. It is a remunerative plan that is compatible with such work concepts as "teams," and "knowledge workers," and "just in time workers" as well as new organizational and operational structures built on the principle of the "virtual organization" and "distributed work." Most importantly, it increases productivity and helps bring down fixed costs. According to a recent survey, approximately 34 percent of the Fortune 1,000 companies are now offering some form of performance reward. The trend is expected to continue and may replace the concept of merit-based pay.[26]

However, any new pay policy usually encounters resistance, and bonuses for productivity concepts do have drawbacks for "not-for-profit" enterprises. A key component of the benefit package is the cash reward. Organizations must be able to generate cash rewards to employees if the concept is to succeed. Academic libraries are not known for having a strong track record when it comes to pay. Second, people who choose a career in the "not-for-profit" sector, while expecting to be paid fairly, are often attracted to an organization because of its cultural tenets and not by pay scales. Underscoring this point is a quote attributed to Michael Moore, the movie director responsible for *Roger & Me,* a humorous 1989 documentary about layoffs at GM. Mr. Moore, who is siding with unionized clerical, maintenance, and dinning hall workers involved in a contract dispute with Yale University, said the following about the dispute:

> You don't want to think of Yale like General Motors. . . . You don't want to think that some of the purpose that the university is structured on is pure greed.[27]

Clearly, redesigning higher education into a more competitive organization would be different for everyone involved and an anathema to those who hold strong convictions that traditional higher education culture is central to the mission of teaching and research.

Nevertheless, several "not-for-profit" enterprises have begun to introduce benefit plans based on the "for-profit" model; chief among these organizations is the American Chemical Society (ACS). The Society stresses membership services and has a distinguished association with educational and scientific organizations. ACS has a membership that includes over 150,000 chemical scientists and engineers. ACS considers itself the world's largest "not-for-profit" scientific society and provides members with an array of services that include publishing, marketing, distribution, program management, research, language translation, information systems technology, meeting planning, and government relations. Other "not-for-profit" organizations looking seriously at the "for-profit" model include heath care and public utility companies.[28,29]

While the concept may be natural for corporations to implement, because they depend on profits to survive, the issue is more complex for units within "not-for-profit" institutions such as academic libraries. The underlying concepts behind reward in a profit motivated operation are dramatically different from the values associated in the "not-for-profit sector." In business, the organizational culture emphasizes and celebrates entrepreneurial success. Employee achievements must be regularly recognized and rewarded in order to retain valuable workers.[30] During the past five years, bonuses in the private sector have become a very popular incentive tool. In 1992, for example, 26 percent of the Fortune 1,000 companies offered bonuses. By 1996 the percentage has increased to 34 percent. During this same period, bonuses became a bigger portion of salaries. In 1993, bonuses awarded to employees in Fortune 1,000 companies represented 4.5 percent of an individual's annual salary compensation package. By 1997, bonuses are projected to represent 7.8 percent of a Fortune 1,000 employee's annual earnings.[31] Academic library directors have never had large sums of discretionary funds available to regularly reward library personnel for notable accomplishments. If pay for performance is to succeed in academic libraries, directors must have the wherewithal to regularly provide monetary incentives, and library personnel must know with confidence that they shall receive more than tea and cookies and a pat on the back when exceptional work is performed.

Despite familiarity with entrepreneurial culture, academic library personnel, like academic faculty, in large measure perceive the business sector to be inferior to traditional collegial environment, even cutthroat, sordid, and inhumane. This strong feeling is exemplified in a recent article in *Library Journal* where the authors question whether the "'soft-edged" service tradition of libraries can "coexist with the 'hard-nosed' entrepreneurial infotech future."[32] There can be no doubt that the comfort level and security for all library personnel, including directors, would be reduced.

Pay concepts, as well as cultural concepts, in higher education libraries are rooted in philosophy based on entitlement. Merit raises and step increases are expected. Job hierarchy, modeled after the hierarchy concepts used by faculty, that is instructor, assistant professor, associate professor and full professor, are widely emulated in academic libraries, often with other nomenclature.

In reward systems truly based on performance, it is the result that is emphasized. Emphasis is placed on the value of the contributions, whether it is individual based or the product of a team project. Unlike academia, job hierarchy is de-emphasized as the basis for remuneration and renown and employees must continually prove themselves and constantly upgrade job skills and knowledge. Longevity as a valued attribute is also less important. In the pay for performance culture, the focus is on career development through the acquisition and application of new knowledge and skills, rather than career development by automatic upward movement. Only exceptional productivity and performance is rewarded by a pay increase above the market level.[33-35]

Major productivity innovations in library operations initiated by academic libraries in the mid-1990s received modest acknowledgment and some surprise from the profession. Rather than celebrating innovation and entrepreneurial initiative, the profession has, to date, overlooked, criticized, and underacknowledged the recent innovations initiated during the 1990s. On the other hand, library outsourcing options initiated by administrators at institutions such as Wright State University and Michigan State University are quietly being adopted by an increasing number of college and university libraries. Failure to acknowledge the risk and celebrate the achievement is difficult to understand and speaks to a flaw in the nature of our profession. Our newfound interest in businesslike approaches to operations is more likely being spurred by what one college administrator purportedly said to a *Chronicle of Higher Education* reporter; that is: "There are 3,600 institutions, and I think 1,000 are going to be out of business in 10 years."[36]

CONCLUSION

The question is no longer whether academic libraries should change, but whether the operational and cultural reforms that are needed can be accomplished from within. Academic libraries, like many consumer businesses in the "for-profit-sector," may expect to experience discomfort as they embark on a transition stage between old and new ways of operating. The challenge for academic library directors is successfully navigating the many risks that await the library business.

NOTES

1. Louis Uchitelle and N. R. Kleinfield, "On the Battlefields of Business, Millions of Casualties," *The New York Times,* 3 March 1996, 14.

2. Ibid., 1.

3. William H. Honan, "Without Money to Build, Western Colleges Innovate to Handle Student Flood," *The New York Times,* 25 September 1996, sec. Education, B6.

4. Frank Emspak, "Both Private and Public Colleges Fight for Financial Health," *The Chronicle of Higher Education,* " 14 June 1996, sec. Special Report, A15.

5. William H. Honan, "New Pressures on the University," *The New York Times,* 9 January 1994, sec. 4A (Educational Life), 16.

6. Shawn Tully, "Finally, Colleges Start To Cut Their Crazy Costs," *Fortune,* 1 May 1995, 110.

7. Christopher Winship and Mark Ratner, "Power of the Pedagogues," *The New York Times,* 17 September 1995, sec. 4 (Week in Review), 15.

8. Honan, "New Pressures on the University," 16.

9. Randy Bradbury, "N.D. University Enrollment: Beyond the Numbers," *Grand Forks Herald,* 27 October 1996, sec. D (Focus), 1D.

10. Honan, "Without Money to Build, Western Colleges Innovate to Handle Student Flood," B9.

11. Peter Drucker, "The Age of Social Transformation," *The Atlantic* 274 (November 1994): 53.

12. Peter J. Denning, "Business Designs for the New University," *Educom Review* 31 (November/December 1996): 20.

13. William H. Honan, "Without Money to Build Western Colleges Innovate to Handle Student Flood," B9.

14. Jeff Livingston, Executive Director for Higher Education Technology & Member of the Western Governors University Design Team, presentation, "Western Governors University–Overview & Progress Report," Libraries and the Western Governors University, August 10, 1996, Marriot Library, University of Utah, Salt Lake City.

15. Tully, "Finally, Colleges Start To Cut Their Crazy Costs," 110.

16. Julie L. Nicklin, "Colleges in Boston to Combine Some Operations to Cut Costs," *The Chronicle of Higher Education,* " 15 April 1996, sec. Business & Philanthropy, A34.

17. Tully, "Finally, Colleges Start To Cut Their Crazy Costs," 110.

18. Honan, "New Pressures on the University," 16.

19. "Governor Enters Fray Over Tenure at U. Of Minnesota," *The Chronicle of Higher Education,* " 11 October 1996, A10.

20. "UM Tenure Talks Moving Slowly," *Grand Forks Herald,* 27 October 1996, sec. B (Region), 7B.

21. Christopher Shea, "At the U. of Rochester, Bad Times Prompt Bold Measures," *The Chronicle of Higher Education,* 15 December 1995, A33.

22. Honan, "New Pressures on the University," 16.

23. "Higher ed by the numbers: 1,2,3," Editorial, *Grand Forks Herald,* 30 September 1996, 4A.

24. Donald C. Bruegman, "An Organizational Model for the 21st Century: Adopting the Corporate Model for Higher Education," *Business Officer: Newsmagazine of the National Association of College and University Business Officers (NACUBO)* 29 (November 1995): 28.

25. Tully, "Finally, Colleges Start To Cut Their Crazy Costs," 110.

26. Barbara B. Buchholz, "The Bonus Isn't Reserved for Big Shots Anymore," *The New York Times,* 27 October 1996, sec. 3 (Money & Business), 10.

27. " 'Corporate Crook of the Year' Dodges Moore," *The Grand Forks Herald,* 1 November 1996, sec. C (Arts & Entertainment), 6C.

28. Ibid., 10.

29. Robert Barner, "The New Millennium Workplace: Seven Changes That Will Challenge Managers–And Workers," *The Futurist,* 30 (March-April 1996): 14.

30. Bruegman, "An Organizational Model for the 21st Century: Adopting the Corporate Model for Higher Education," 28.

31. Buchholz, "The Bonus Isn't Reserved for Big Shots Anymore," 10.

32. Sheila Bertram and Hope Olson, "Culture Clash," *Library Journal* 121 (15 October 1996): 36.

33. Christopher M. Lowery, M. M. Petty, and James W. Thompson, "Employee Perceptions of the Effectiveness of a Performance-Based Pay Program in a Large Public Utility," *Public Personnel Management* 24 (Winter 1995): 475.

34. Norman E. Bowie, "The Clash Between Academic Values and Business Values, *Business & Professional Ethics Journal* 12 (Winter 1993): 3.

35. Sally B. Bailery and Howard Risher, " 'If The Shoe Fits': Not-for-Profits Try Out New Compensation Plans," *Compensation & Benefits Review,* 28 (May/June 1996): 47.

36. Patrick Healy, Kit Lively, Joyce Mercer, Julie Nicklin, and Peter Schmidt, "Both Private and Public Colleges Fight for Financial Health," *The Chronicle of Higher Education,* 14 June 1996, sec. Special Report, A15.

Index

Acting directors. *See* Library
    directors, acting or interim
Affirmative action, 32,34-35
Age, of library directors, 39
Airline industry, organizational
    changes in, 89
Alaska, University of, at Fairbanks,
    as COSUL member, 36,37
American Association of Higher
    Education,
    Teaching-Learning-and-
    Technology Roundtable, 67
American Chemical Society, 96
Arkansas, University of, as COSUL
    member, 36,37
Arkansas State University, as
    COSUL member, 36,37
Associated Colleges of the Midwest,
    81
Associate library directors, 11-12
Association of American Colleges,
    76
Association of Colleges and
    Research Libraries
    (ACRL), 67
Association of Research Libraries
    (ARL). *See also* Council on
    State University Libraries
    (COSUL)
    library directorships of, 77
    acting directors, 26
    female, 32-33,34
    male, 43
Attention, management of, 55
Authority
    in academic environment, 85
    of acting library directors, 5
Automobile industry, organizational
    change in, 89,90

Baby-boom generation, 90-91
Bonuses, 95-96,97
Boston, Fenway-district colleges of,
    92-93
Bridge Over the River Kwai (movie),
    21
Business model, of fiscal policies, 2,
    94-98

California, University of
    post-World War II expansion of, 90
    proposed faculty reductions by,
    93
    Study of the Academic Profession
    by, 80
California State University,
    post-World War II
    expansion of, 90
Carnegie Classification for
    Educational Institutions, 37
Carnegie Foundation, 76
Carnegie Foundation for the
    Advance of Teaching, 74
Cataloging, 64
Change
    initiation by acting library
    directors, 5
    management of, 3,49,54-55
    organizational, 48,89,90-91
    faculty's resistance to, 92
    library director's role in, 56
    organizations' response to,
    47-48
    relationship to leadership, 4,53
    strategic, 54
    rate of, 4
City University of New York,
    proposed faculty reductions
    by, 93

College and Research Libraries,
   50-51
Colleges. *See also names of specific*
   colleges
   fiscal policies of, 89-100
     administrative reorganization,
       62
     business model of, 2,94-98
     effect of consumer demands
       on, 48,49,91
     effect of overexpansion on,
       90-91
     external influences on, 91-92,
       93-94
     legislative restrictions on,
       91-92,94
     performance-based wage
       policies, 95-98
     revenue-generating strategies,
       92
     tenure issue in, 92,93-94
   funding of
     decreased sources of, 89
     legislative restrictions on, 91
     in New England, 62
   not-for-profit orientation of, 92
   organizational change by, 48,54,
     56,89,90-91
   predicted closure of, 98
   public's changing expectations of,
     48
College students
   changing demographics of, 91
   as consumers, 48,49,91
Communication skills
   of acting library directors, 13-14
   of leaders, 55
   of library directors, 79
Community, as academic ethic
   in liberal arts colleges, 75-76,78,
     81-82,83-84,86
   in research universities, 80,81
Competition, individual, 53
Computer technology. *See*
   Information technology

Consensus-building, by acting
   library directors, 15,22
Consolidation, of services, 92-93
COSUL. *See* Council on State
   University Libraries
Consumer industries, profit-related
   changes in, 89
Consumerism, 48,49,91
Council on State University Libraries
   (COSUL)
   library directors' succession patterns
     survey of, 31-32,35-44
   directors' average age, 39
   directors' education, 38-39
   directors' professional
     experience, 42
   directors' tenure status, 39-41
   internal versus external
     succession patterns, 41
   in rural versus urban colleges,
     43-44
   statistics on, 37-38
Culture, organizational, 11,54,55

Deans
   at Harvard University, 84-85
   of liberal arts colleges, 77,79
   as library directors, 26,77,79
   at University of Rhode Island,
     60-71
Deputy library directors, 11. *See also*
   Library directors, acting or
   interim
Directors. *See* Library directors
Distance learning, 50,91-92
Doctorates, held by library directors,
   39,65

Earlham College, 82
Eastern Educational Research
   Association, 45
Electronic document delivery, 92
Electronic management report
   systems, 95

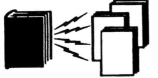

Haworth
DOCUMENT DELIVERY
SERVICE

This valuable service provides a single-article order form for any article from a Haworth journal.

- *Time Saving:* No running around from library to library to find a specific article.
- *Cost Effective:* All costs are kept down to a minimum.
- *Fast Delivery:* Choose from several options, including same-day FAX.
- *No Copyright Hassles:* You will be supplied by the original publisher.
- *Easy Payment:* Choose from several easy payment methods.

Open Accounts Welcome for ...
- Library Interlibrary Loan Departments
- Library Network/Consortia Wishing to Provide Single-Article Services
- Indexing/Abstracting Services with Single Article Provision Services
- Document Provision Brokers and Freelance Information Service Providers

---

MAIL or *FAX* THIS ENTIRE ORDER FORM TO:

Haworth Document Delivery Service
The Haworth Press, Inc.
10 Alice Street
Binghamton, NY 13904-1580

or FAX: 1-800-895-0582
or CALL: 1-800-342-9678
9am-5pm EST

PLEASE SEND ME PHOTOCOPIES OF THE FOLLOWING SINGLE ARTICLES:

1) Journal Title: _____
    Vol/Issue/Year: _____ Starting & Ending Pages: _____
Article Title: _____
_____

2) Journal Title: _____
    Vol/Issue/Year: _____ Starting & Ending Pages: _____
Article Title: _____
_____

3) Journal Title: _____
    Vol/Issue/Year: _____ Starting & Ending Pages: _____
Article Title: _____
_____

4) Journal Title: _____
    Vol/Issue/Year: _____ Starting & Ending Pages: _____
Article Title: _____
_____

(See other side for Costs and Payment Information)

COSTS: Please figure your cost to order quality copies of an article.

1. Set-up charge per article: $8.00
   ($8.00 × number of separate articles) _____

2. Photocopying charge for each article:

   1-10 pages: $1.00 _____

   11-19 pages: $3.00 _____

   20-29 pages: $5.00 _____

   30+ pages: $2.00/10 pages _____

3. Flexicover (optional): $2.00/article _____

4. Postage & Handling: US: $1.00 for the first article/
   $.50 each additional article _____

   Federal Express: $25.00 _____

   Outside US: $2.00 for first article/
   $.50 each additional article _____

5. Same-day FAX service: $.35 per page _____

GRAND TOTAL: _____

METHOD OF PAYMENT: (please check one)

❑ Check enclosed ❑ Please ship and bill. PO # _____
(sorry we can ship and bill to bookstores only! All others must pre-pay)

❑ Charge to my credit card: ❑ Visa; ❑ MasterCard; ❑ Discover;
❑ American Express;

Account Number: _____ Expiration date: _____

Signature: ✗ _____

Name: _____ Institution: _____

Address: _____

_____

City: _____ State: _____ Zip: _____

Phone Number: _____ FAX Number: _____

MAIL or *FAX* THIS ENTIRE ORDER FORM TO:

Haworth Document Delivery Service	**or FAX:** 1-800-895-0582
The Haworth Press, Inc.	**or CALL:** 1-800-342-9678
10 Alice Street	9am-5pm EST)
Binghamton, NY 13904-1580	